Singing Stream's Tarot

by

Laurie White

Singing Stream's Tarot

For information address
fromlauriewhite@gmail.com

First Printing 2024

ISBN: 987-0-6459672-7-2

Acknowledgements

Here I wish to acknowledge my teachers and trainers, and the inherent wisdom buried in my DNA from my ancestors.

My Teachers: Gloria Romanic of Horseshoe Valley Ontario Canada. Suzanne Nadon, Owen Sound Ontario Canada, Sandra Ingerman and Michael Harner of the Foundation of Shamanic Studies, California USA, Brooke Medicine Eagle, Montana USA, Jamie Sams California USA, and every single participant that has attended my Circles and gifted me with their truth, their teachings.

All the Women and Men that have attended my Drumming Circles, Healing Circles and Weekend Workshops over the last four decades both in Ontario Canada, and Nova Scotia Canada.

I wish to thank my friend Michael Davies for all his help in getting this project going, and for his guidance and patience in getting me here. This undertaking wouldn't be a reality at all without his brilliance and his caring. Thank you, Michael.

Blessed Be

Dedications

This work is dedicated to My Daughter Cindy Hill for her undying support regarding the decision to move forward for the creation of this Tarot Card Book and set of Cards.

and

To my Soul Mate, my dear Husband, my Best Friend and Lover for all his patience and encouragement moving through this process, and his unwavering support and love in all I do.

and

To every single Woman and Man that have attended my Circles and Workshops over the years. For all their teachings while holding the Talking Stick.

Their encouragement and support, pushing me to attended workshops myself to study and learn more

and more techniques to teach in our Circles.

Thank you all from the bottom of my Heart.

Preface

I was born and raised in Toronto Ontario, and I was blessed to receive my guidance largely through my Grandmother and Grandfather. They raised me in the church, providing a strong faith foundation for me. Had I not had that firm foundation, when I fell to my knees, many times in adulthood, I don't believe I would have been able to get back up, dust myself off, and move forward. I always believed that the Creator helps those that help themselves.

In my 74th year now, it has occurred to me that I won't live forever, and the one thing I don't want to do is leave this world without leaving all I've studied, learned, and taught in my counselling career, behind. I wanted to find a way to share my teachings to help others on their healing journey. Offering Tarot readings was one of the tools I used along with Women's and mixed Healing Circles, Drumming Circles as well as Weekend Workshops. My studies included North American Native Spirituality, Shamanic Healing techniques, Women's Studies, Pagan, Wicca and Earth Religions. I hold great respect for the Native Medicine Wheel and the wisdom of the Good Red Road I've learned there.

A Native Elder once told me the very best way to form your own faith is to learn other ones that resonate with you and then come home with that wisdom and create your own. My way of knowing then exists through all the teachings I've gathered, not instead of my base faith, but as well as. When I returned to my base way of knowing I was blessed to meet a Spiritual Leader that answered all my questions. That made sense of many things I didn't understand before. For her, I will always be grateful. Finding an open faith family that accepted me for exactly who I am, and was created to be, fed my soul. I was able to share all that I know to be true to the Church's women's group. I was able to share Healing Circles, Drumming Circles, Tarot Readings, and ways to make wild herb salves and tinctures and teas, and much more.

In 1991 I had the privilege of giving back to the Native Women of Rama Reserve in Ontario. I'll never forget the day I gave them back their own Creation Story. The tears poured down my face as I told them the story of Sky Woman. Rama's Chief told me, "When our women become strong again, we will be okay."

This year, 2024, on October 25th I will celebrate fifty years Sobriety and as you can imagine, this has provided me with a wealth of knowledge. As well as being a Recovering Alcoholic, I am also the only child of an abusive alcoholic. Over the years I have had a private practice as an Addiction Educational Consultant and I worked at the Addiction Research Foundation, and at a Halfway House for men that were coming off skid row, following a dry out period at a detox center. I had a case load of eight to ten men and held the daily counselling meetings for all the residents, as well as the weekly AA meetings.

My Healing Circles were held weekly and for some time there were four different locations that I travelled to.

My hope for coming to readers with this book is to bring the wisdom of the Ancients to many. Knowledge that will sustain everyone that has this book, and these Tarot Cards, helping them navigate their Healing Journey.

So Mote It Be

Singing Stream

Card Index

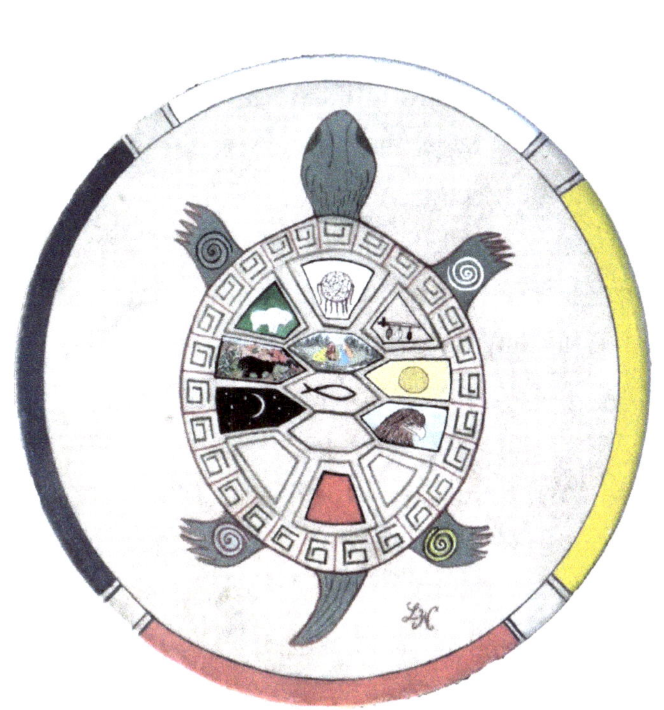

1. Peace Pipe

First Nations people tell the story of how the Peace Pipe came to the people. It is said that two young male hunters saw, in the distance, what appeared to be a White Buffalo Calf on the horizon. As the calf came closer it transformed into a Woman in a beautiful long white cape. One of the young men had bad thoughts about this Woman, in the middle of nowhere, by herself...and his intent turned to taking advantage of her. He began to approach her with ill intent and so she opened her cape to receive him. The young man walked right up to her and she draped her cape around him. When she opened her cape again, the young man was nothing but a pile of ashes in front of White Buffalo Calf Woman. She told the other young man, watching on in amazement, that 'she arrived to give the Peace Pipe to his people, that there would be no more war and turmoil on Earth.' She told him to 'go back to his people's camp and report her arrival.' The young man did as she asked.

When she arrived at the camp she spoke to the people and asked that they lay down their weapons and maintain Peace upon the Earth. She presented the Peace Pipe to the Chief and told him to use the pipe in ceremony and in all counsel gatherings, and to burn sacred raw tobacco in the pipe. She told the

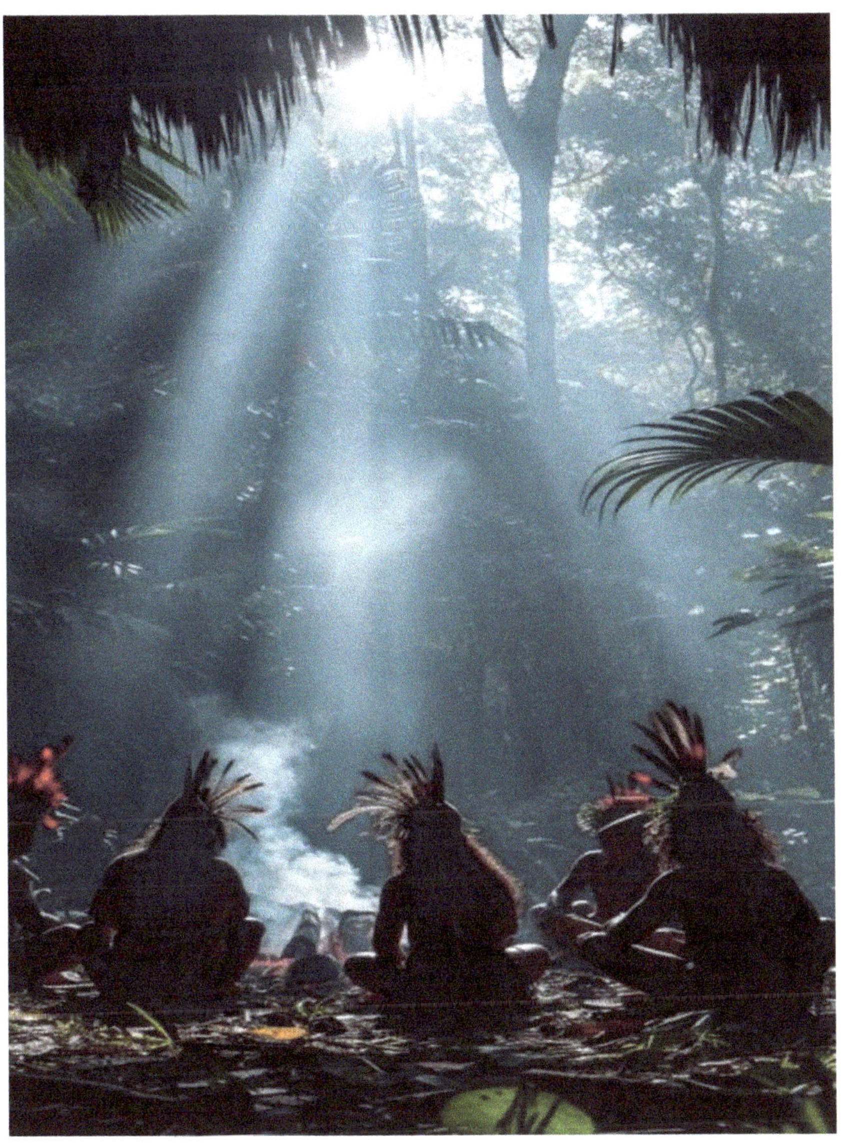

Chief to appoint one person to be the Pipe Carrier. So it was. She turned to leave, and as she did, she gradually transformed into a White Buffalo Calf once again.

Application

We are well aware of the places in our lives where we do not feel that peace resides. White Buffalo Calf Woman's message is clear, it is up to us to create the peace that we long for. Our intent must be clear and uncluttered, our weapons laid down.

Forgiveness, as well, is called for here, being aware that forgiveness isn't especially for the offender, but for giving to yourself. Prayer is also called for when creating Peace. Prayer to the Universe, to the Creator of all things...whatever form that takes for you. Be the Peace you wish to see in our World.

Make me a channel of your Peace,
Where there is hatred let me bring your Love,
Where there is injury your pardon Creator,
And where there's doubt true faith in you.

Make me a channel of your Peace,
Where there's despair in Life let me bring hope
And where there's Darkness, only Light
And where there's sadness ever Joy.

Oh Creator grant that I may never seek,
So much to be consoled as to console,
To be understood as to understand,
To be loved as to love with all my soul.

2. Consulting Self

When we consult Self we reach for our preferred Divination tool whether that be your Tarot Card Deck or Rune Stones perhaps, or both. Either way you want to prepare the area where you wish to work. It's important to mark this sacred space in time by creating sacred ground, in a place where you won't be interrupted.

You want to choose a card that will speak to that which you have focused on while choosing it. Sometimes, the Universe will decide that there is something more pressing than the question you have come with. In that event you will receive the card that the Universe feels you need to digest first. Trust.

It's always important to realize that the power that brings your answers to you isn't the cards. The power is you. The cards are simply a tool like the candle, the smouldering sage, the soft music playing, that assist you in connecting your heart with the heart of the force that created you.

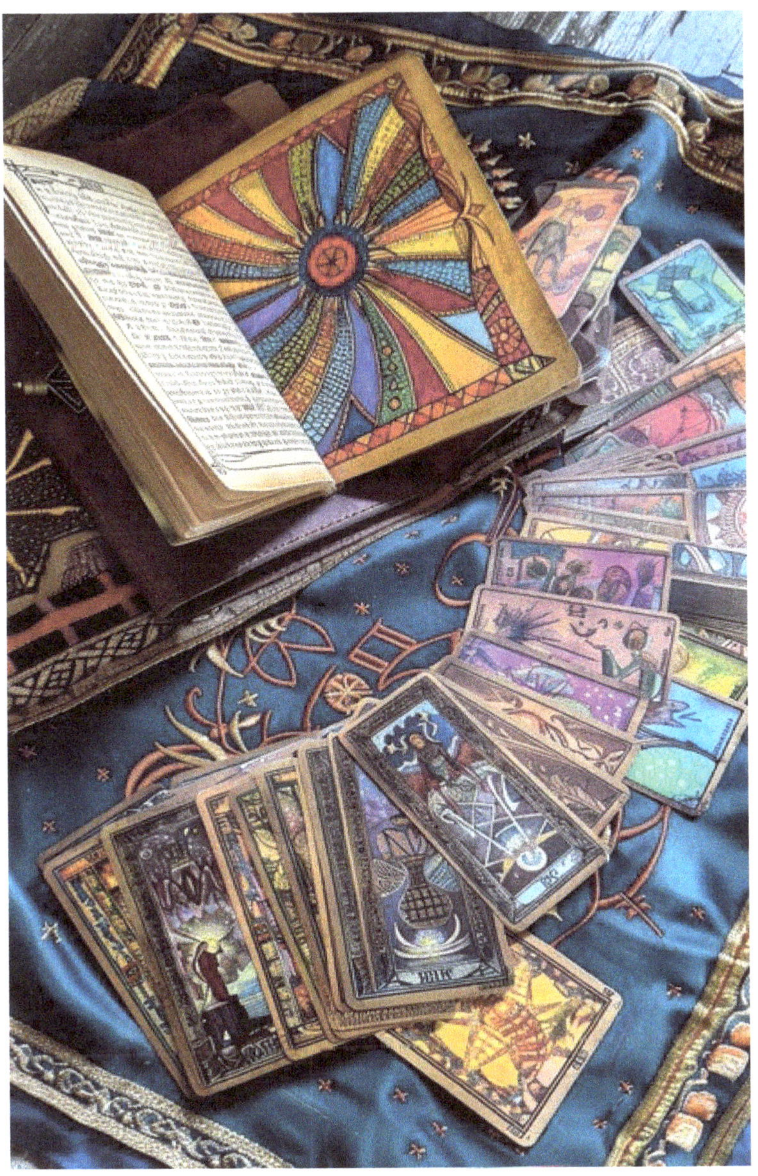

You do that by clearing that pathway of clutter, whether that's 'the things you feel you need to do after this consultation' or 'your grocery shopping list' or whatever or whoever else creeps into your mind from time to time.

Focus only on what it is you wish to hear about. You are the power here. Just you. The clearer you are of clutter, by gifting yourself with the tools, that create sacred ground for you... remaining focused, the clearer your reading will be.

Focus, while your hand hovers over the cards, moving left to right, using your left hand, your female side, your 'information coming in' side. You will feel a shift in energy on the palm of your hand when you are over the right card. Some people feel a tingle, some, a change in temperature, or simply a knowing...trust, that you can not pick the wrong card. When you take your hand away your card is the one that you believe it is. You will recognize the card's teaching, correlating with your focus going into the reading, immediately...the minute you start reading. If the Universe has decided on another choice for you, that is critical that you hear before the thing or things you were focusing on, you will recognize what that is, the moment you begin reading.

There is no right way or wrong way to give yourself or someone else a reading. Experiment to find what really feels right, and brings your peace home, to you.

My forte' is teaching Women's Spirituality and touches many ways of knowing on our planet. Earth Religion, Paganism, Wicca, Goddess Religion, Buddhism, Nature Spirituality, North American Native Spirituality and the teachings of the Medicine Wheel of Life to name a few. Whatever speaks to, and provides peace with teachings that lift you into a higher level of consciousness, these are the divination cards for you now.

And know...

You are a being of Pure White Light.
You are a being of Pure White Light.
Only good can come to you.
Only good can move through you.
Only good, can be here.

Application

When you receive this card in a reading it signals that it is indeed time to live and learn an experience that will give you the answers you seek. A belief system that gives you more depth, and understandable meaning. When our belief system leaves us with some voids, empty spaces, unanswered questions....confusion, and we innately know 'there's more', there just has to be, this practice will literally bring you to your wisdom.

The wisdom within you, the wisdom of your ancestors is there for you to access at any time. Over time as we give and do for others in our lives, we feel blessed, elated in having helped them, but, our vessel empties if we go without nurturing ourselves. It is our responsibility to take the steps needed to refill our own vessels. If, like myself, it is the woods for example, that feeds you, that immediately moves you to breathe deeper and think clearer, then go there to refill. Breathe in through your nose, and out through your mouth....lengthening the breaths in, and the breaths out. Be with your dear self and take in the beauty and the bounty of our home and our oneness with Mother Earth and all that is.

Bring your fullness back to your life, being even richer than before. You win, and everyone else in your world wins....and Mother Earth wins too, when we take the time to consult self.

3. Healing Circle

There was a time when I was hosting four Healing Circles per week, in different locations. Workshop weekends were popular too with women, so I hosted four per year celebrating the Solstices and the Equinoxes. When the Women arrived, for any and all gatherings, I always had Chai tea simmering on the stove, that included cardamon seeds, believed to open you up. Women would gather and right on time, I signaled that it was time to move to the healing room, with a song. Often, we had twenty-five women in attendance. We'd form a Circle sitting on the floor, cross legged. The candles would be lit by the women, in the direction of the room that they felt most drawn to that night. These women were seasoned in the Medicine Wheel Teachings, the knowledge of changing feelings, characteristics that matched the attributes of any one direction at that time. We sat and took hands, left palm (your 'information coming in side') facing upwards and right palm ('your information going out side') facing downwards, allowing the energy to flow freely.

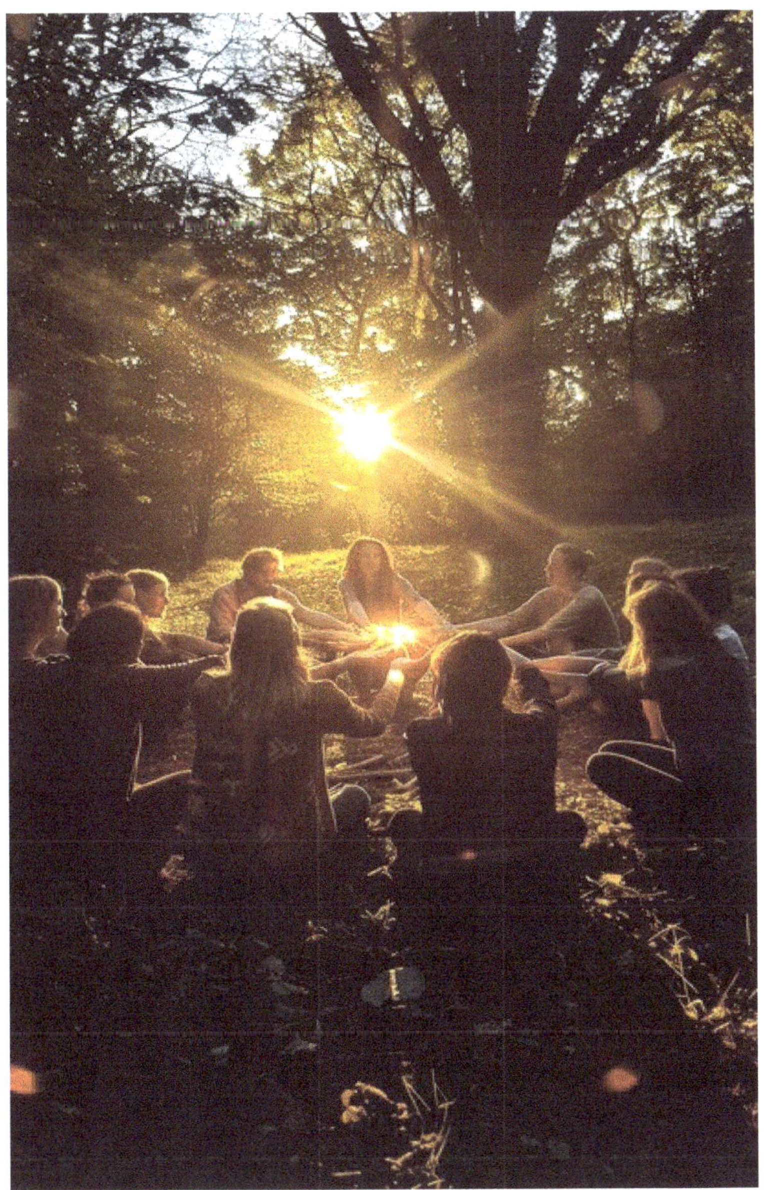

We sang a familiar chant together called "The Greatest Mystery." Then we checked in with each other, shared any business and new endeavours by certain woman, getting clear of any small talk. We smudged with sage, one by one while raising energy and cleansing our auras of any debris that may collect as we move through our days. We smudged with sage, one by one while raising energy and cleansing our auras of any debris that may collect as we move through our days. We create sacred ground. As the smudge was passed, each woman looked into the eyes of the other and said, "I honour your journey, I honour your truth." It was at this time, we then spoke about It was at this time, we then spoke about confidentiality being assured, for all. We created sacred ground..We would share in a meditation, then I would offer a teaching. Some would refill their teacups at this point and we would proceed by a woman using our Talking Stick and speaking about something that has been affecting her. This could be something bad, or something joyful, or something in between. She will speak her words openly and with amazing confidence that she is being fully heard, held in love and respect, and assisted in every way possible. There are never any judgments made when she lowers the stick back into place and lets go of it. The only comments that will come her way are from those that have walked exactly the same path and will share their way of handling it for themselves. Everyone's words spoken with the Talking Stick are considered to be that woman's teachings. We thank her for her teachings. And if there is anything we can do to support her and take away her fear we will. For example one night the Circle offered to assist a woman whose voice was rarely acknowledged, who had been assaulted. She laid in the center of the Circle and we moved in closer to her. Our finger tips barely touching her (with her permission of course) we began to make sounds. We opened our mouths and started softly whisper yelling. She joins us. We eventually got louder, and even louder...before you know it we were screaming and she joined in, for as long as she wanted to. It was so amazingly healing for her!

Sometimes, no one takes the Talking Stick. Generally on these occasions, I bring out the Tarot Cards and everyone chooses one. We go around the Circle and express how the card they chose resonates with them now. This too opens women up that really need to open. In a trusting Healing Circle, the women will get restless, they'll tire, if someone is taking the stick in their hands and repeating the same thing each and every time. When it's obvious that the woman isn't moving forward with that matter at all, the women in the Circle will tell her. Then we can get down to business. Let the Healing begin! We end the Circle when everything feels finished for all who are there.

Application

In Ancient times, Women always had a place where they would be heard, respected, honored, and believed to carry great wisdom within. These are the places we must create in our lives if they aren't there. In this day and age many women do what women have always done...they give, do, nurture, organize and fulfill their obligations to the best of their ability. We have given and given and given until our vessels are empty. The place that you can easily refill your vessel, firstly, must be known to you, and be accessible to you at all times. This is a woman's responsibility to know where to go, and go and do it. Women always gathered at the New Moon to refill. This was a way of life....not a matter of whether you can make it or not. Every 28 days refilling, renewing, gaining more and more ancient wisdom from the Crones, the Elders...and the visions they gained in the Moon Lodge was hungered for by the men of the tribes, so they would know what to do and how to act out. The men spent the time praying in the Sweat Lodge when the women were absent each New Moon, for three days. When the three days ended the men waited patiently for the Life Givers to return with direction for the next Moon cycle. Where to move, what to hunt next and where, and even, who will live in what long house...everything. If the Healing Circle card has floated into your spread today it's time to find your peace, your Healing Circle. If you can't find one, start one in your community. Time to refill your vessel. Time to renew yourself in order to easily navigate for the next moon cycle.

The Circle is Open
But Never Broken
May the Grace of the Goddess
Go With Us in Our Hearts
Merry Meet, Merry Part
And Merry Meet Again
Blessed Be

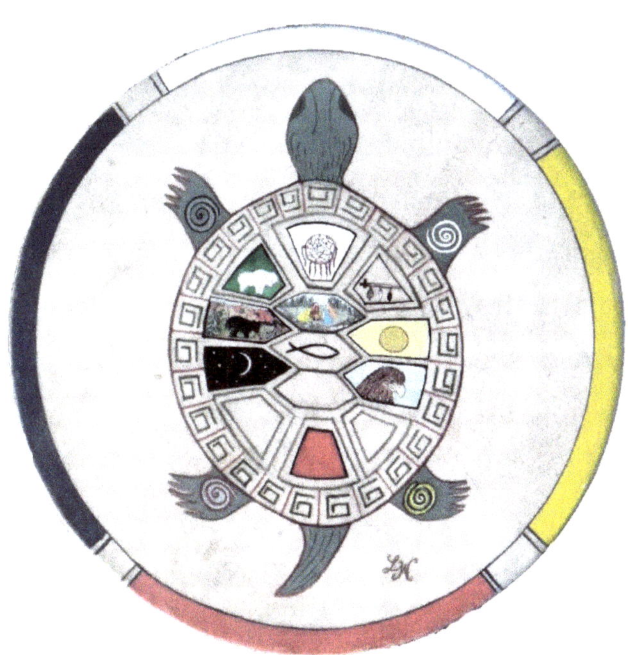

4. Talking Stick

A Talking Stick is a sacred tool used in Talking Circles, Healing Circles, Drumming Circles, or for anyone in your home including Children, or in any other ceremony. The idea is to set your talking stick in the center of the Circle and when one of the Circle participants feels they have something they would like to speak to...sometimes for support, for ideas of how to handle a situation, or just to express a feeling as a sharing...whatever the reason, the one that holds the talking stick in a sacred and trusting circle is the only one that speaks. After they feel finished speaking, they will lay the talking stick back into the center of the Circle. If someone would like to speak to the words spoken by the participant, they must remember there are no judgements made in any of these ceremonies...one must only speak to their own experience on the matter. For this to happen that person will pick up the Answering Feather. No one else speaks while they hold the feather. Once either the Talking Stick or the Answering Feather is returned to the center of the Circle someone else may wish to share her teachings with the Circle.

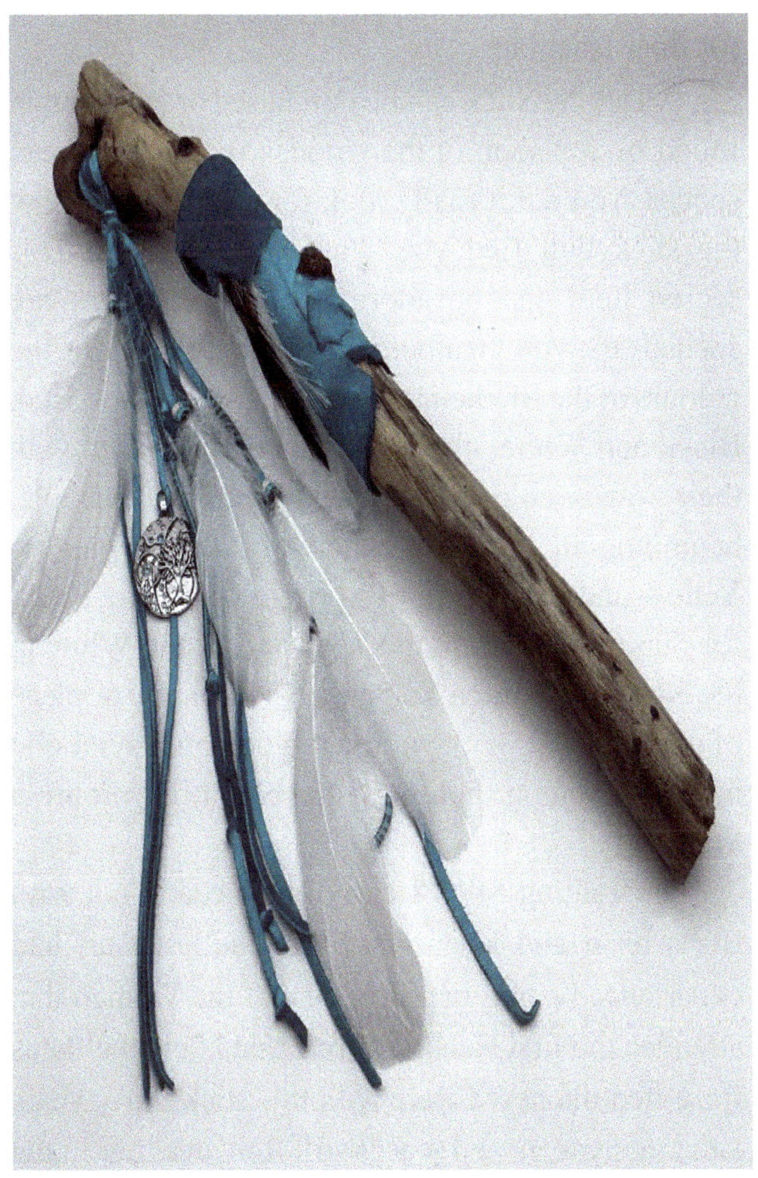

We see everything that someone shares as their teaching to us. Often people will thank that person for their teaching.

A Talking Stick can be purchased or even better, found by a person in the woods...forests...or green spaces. You don't really look for a stick, know that the stick will find you. You won't miss it. This sacred item can be adorned with items that are special to you...feathers, crystals, beads in the colours of the Medicine Wheel of Life. Yellow, Red, Black and White...the four races of man, each with their own colour and season. For example, beginning in the East, where the day begins, is Yellow and the season of Spring. Red in the South for Summer, Black in the West in Fall and White in the North for Winter. You may have a fabric or piece of moss maybe, with your last blood on it symbolic of your Croning, holding your blood, if you are a Woman.

The Talking Stick I carry is a Cedar Root with Burls on it and at one end the smallest Burl had experienced being in a fire. One of the Women that attended the first Healing Circle that I held the focus for gifted the new Circle with this stick. forty years later, many tears and words still flow over her in the Circle.

Application

When you draw the Talking Stick card to you in a reading it signals a time for you to open up to someone you trust deeply, and express that which you need to speak about. Whether it is about finances, relationships, children, your work outside the home, your unfulfilled needs, dieting, or anything heavy on your mind and heart. If it is a burden you carry, certainly a trusted Healing Circle will hold you up by supporting anything you wish. We will hold a vision with you for your dreams to manifest...anything. Collectively the members of your Circle, or that single Spiritual friend will cradle you and help you draw your desired outcomes to you.

If you are a silent screamer, someone that gives her/his power away by never speaking up, your selected listener will scream with you for as long as it takes to unblock that passage. Just know, you are being put on notice now to address your concerns and relieve your heart...creating space for all that is meaningful, spiritual, and blessed.

****

5. Herbal Walks

With my Field Guide in hand off I went to the woods. I wouldn't travel very far before I'd spy a plant that intrigued me. One of the first was the Trout Lily. It presents a lovely small yellow lily like flower, about a 3 1/2" stem and short tulip like leaves resembling a camo pattern, in early Spring. The medicinal quality they have is that the leaves, once dried by tribal women, when chewed on, provided a contraceptive they could rely on. It was never wise to birth a child in the harsh Winter months. These beautiful little Lily-like flowers are one of the first flora in early Spring, proceeded only by Colt's Foot flowers that arrive first, even before its leaves appear. The leaves are shaped like the outline of a Colt's Foot, ergo the name. The Medicinal quality in these pretty little yellow flowers is that, dried and smoked, would remove mucus from the lungs. Prepared as a tea, or a salve they were also used to treat respiratory conditions such as gout, flu, colds, and fever. It helps condition the skin and reduces the oxidative stress on it. Colts Foot safeguards against microbial function and makes the skin look younger.

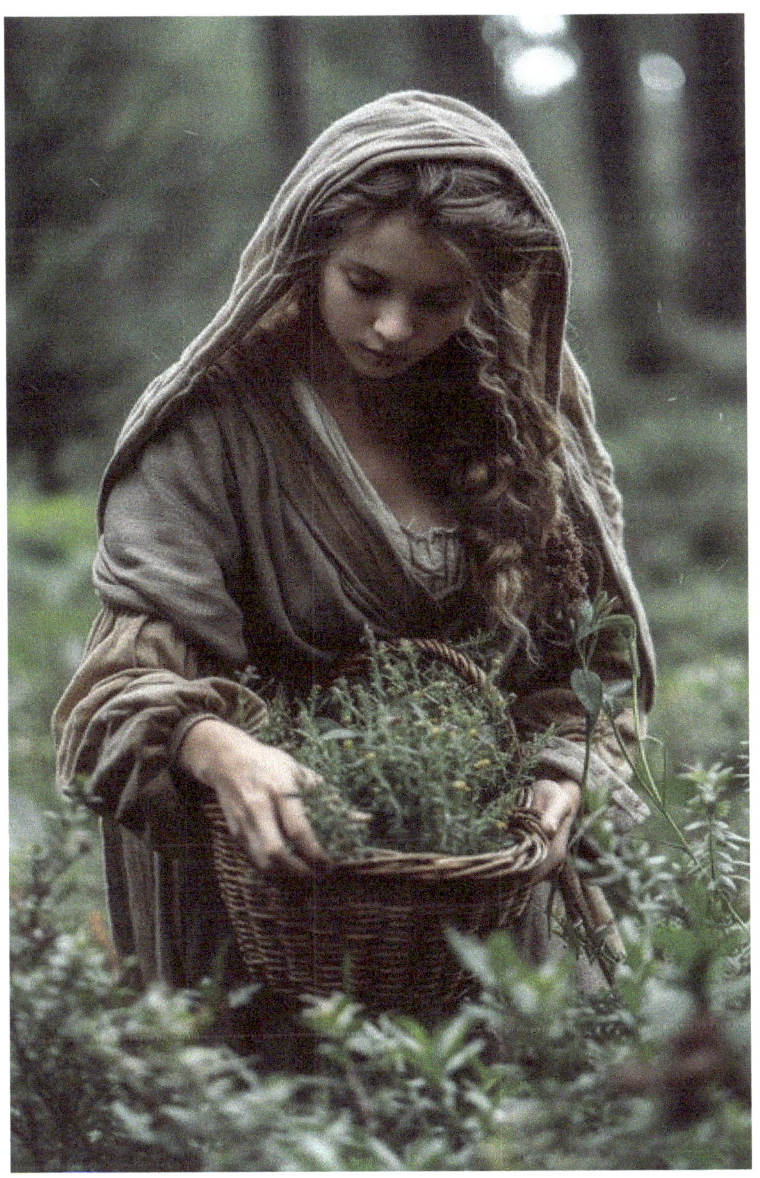

Labrador Tea is a short shrub that enjoys acidic soil and intrigues by presenting green leather looking lance shaped leaves with a distinguished soft light brown suede looking underside that is harvested in the Spring before the white clustered flowers appear, and tribal people used it to treat respiratory, digestive and kidney problems as well as rheumatism, scurvy and headaches; it was also used as a blood purifier and to ease labor. Boneset is another interesting wild herb. Characterized by the way the stems pierce the leaves, dividing the leaf on the left and right of the stem and joined as one leaf. Boneset won its amazing name due to its magical power of setting the bones when wrapped with the bandages around a splint.

So you see, much knowledge can be gained just by walking and observing all the lovely little plants and bushes in nature. From the Spring of the year to the Fall, each plant came up to be harvested either by drying or using fresh, keeping the tribal people busy during Spring, Summer and Fall gathering medicinal herbs. Each one in due time, all in their specific areas in the woodlands and meadows.

When being harvested, tribal people didn't rape areas of any one herb. They always were mindful to leave two-thirds of each plant, so there would be a continuance of these medicines for the next seven generations. May It Continue to Be So!!!

Application

This card is coming to you now to inform you of all the medicines that are available for you and your family, and your community, as well as the global family for many generations to come. The plants in your own yard for example are only there because you need them. For example, should you or someone you love be suffering with depression, St. John's Wort will appear near you, and so on.

You are being reminded that our Mother the Earth provides any and all that you need to survive. All that is required is that you learn about them, and their precautions, interactions, as well as their medicinal qualities and how to prepare each one….their uses and whether you use the whole plant including the roots, or just some of it. Whether you make a salve, tincture, wash, or tea….This card reminds you that most pharmaceuticals are derived from the plants provided by our Earth. Learn about them, and use with caution and with assurance that when our Mother the Earth is honoured and respected, she will always provide and renew.

You must become proactive in the protection of our waters, our rain forests, our air and woodlands, for the good of All Our Relations. (Two legged, four legged, swimmers, winged ones, crawlers, forests and air we breathe.) Blessed Be!

The Earth is our Mother
We must take care of her
The Earth is our Mother
We must take care of her.
Unite my people, be ONE,
Unite my people, be ONE.
Her sacred ground we walk upon
With every step we take,
Her sacred ground we walk upon
With every step we take.
Unite my people, be ONE
Unite my people, be ONE.

6. Unconditional Love

Understanding Unconditional Love came early in my world. My Grandfather showed it to me, and he continued to do so until I lost him when I was twenty-two. I understand now, why I basically died with him, for I didn't feel that love again until I married my best friend at the age of fifty-three. It was my children's Grandmother that snapped me out of my absence from the world around me, pointing out that I had a little girl depending on my full attention...not just a shell of a woman going through the motions. My Grandfather also portrayed the light of 'Hope' to me as well. He and my Grandmother made sure I had strong Faith in a loving and forgiving Creator. Certainly without this I wouldn't have gotten up, when I fell to my knees many times throughout the years. This is an important message to all parents, to be sure that your small children have a strong Faith in whatever your faith formation may have been, or still is.

Unconditional Love can be explained as a knowing within you that no matter what happens in your life, that a deep abiding love will always be with you no matter what happens.

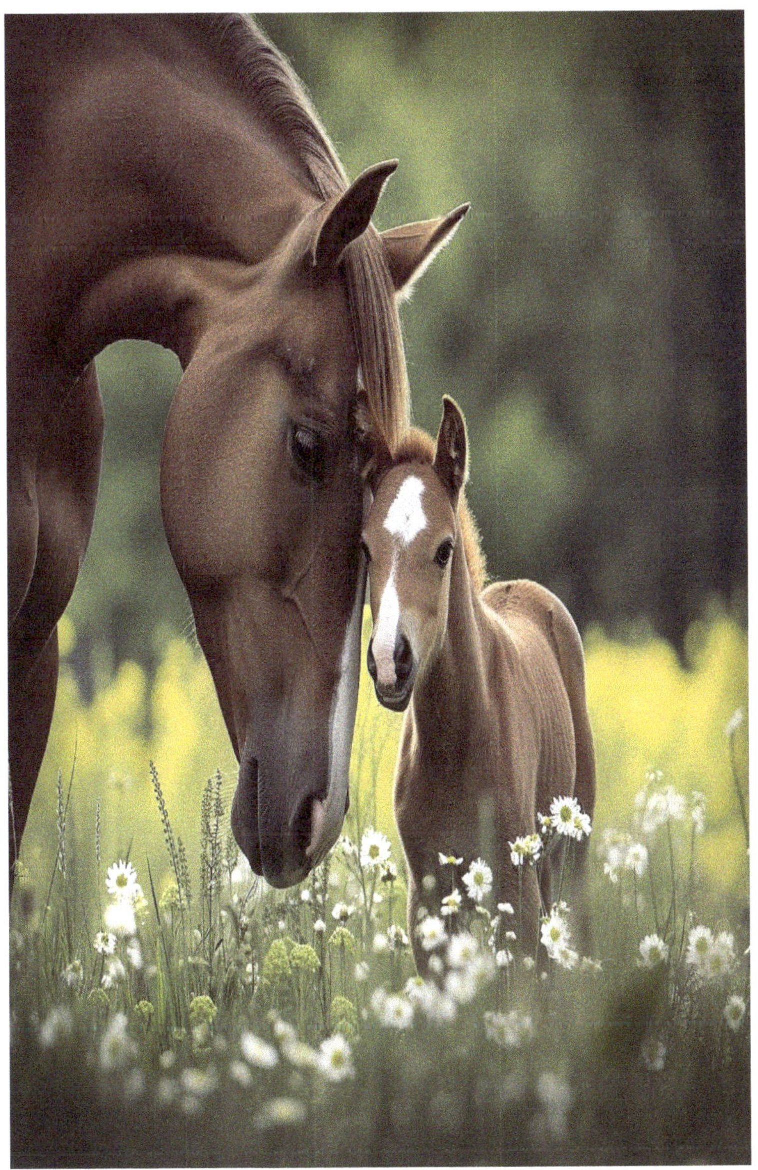

A love that means you love a person or other living being and expect nothing in return but their happiness.

Although infinite and measureless, Unconditional love separates the individual from their behaviour. However, the individual may exhibit behaviours that are unacceptable in a particular situation.

A perfect example of Unconditional Love would be the love given to you by your Dog. When you spell Dog backwards it equals God. Is it any wonder?

Application

It is one thing to give love, but to love unconditionally, is really love given at a whole other level. If you are sure of Love in your life but question if it is conditional or unconditional it's time to confront that, and sort it to your acceptance. An example might be that you continue to love a person, but not unconditionally any longer, after you have experienced abuse from this person. If this is the case ask yourself if you are, in turn, loved conditionally by this person.

Giving Unconditional Love to yourself is required in all cases. The way to do so and continue to do so is, one has to walk in beauty with the force that created us, with the natural world, and with all living things within it. Feed your love for yourself with that which sustains you, regularly. Never put what nourishes and nurtures you on the back burner. Be kind with yourself, in all ways. Take time for YOU, Unconditionally!

Walk in Beauty, it's all around you,
Walk in Beauty, let Love surround you,
Walk in Beauty, make it around you,
Walk in Beauty, with love for all.

Walk in Beauty, it's all around you,
Walk Earth with honour, shine love upon her,
Walk in Beauty sweet Earth we honour,
Walk in Beauty with love for all.

Brook Medicine Eagle

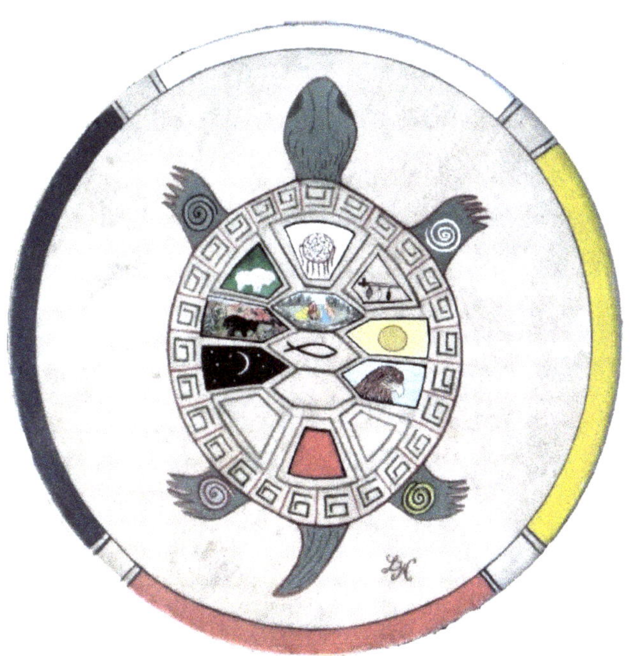

7. Sweat Lodge

The third last Sweat Lodge I taught and held, the focus for was just before I left Ontario to live in Nova Scotia. There were thirty participants and we all stayed in cabins on the property we rented in Gravenhurst. We began our workshop weekend on Friday night, constructing a huge Medicine Wheel with rocks...each spoke had its own meaning, as well as each rock. In the center of the wheel was the fire, known as the Creator. This wheel was the space we spent the whole weekend in when we worked. This was the space we used to build our Sweat Lodge in on Saturday afternoon, to partake of at dark, on Saturday evening.

We ate a late lunch together, and then fasted until after the lodge was over, when we enjoyed a huge (planned) feast. In the afternoon the construction of the lodge began. The Sweat Lodge is fashioned as the body of a turtle, and known as the womb of Mother Earth. The fire in the center of the Medicine Wheel is known as the head of the turtle, the walkway into where we crawl into the lodge is known as the turtle's neck. The mound of soil just to the right of the door to the lodge is soil taken out of the center of the lodge where the hot lava rocks will be placed.

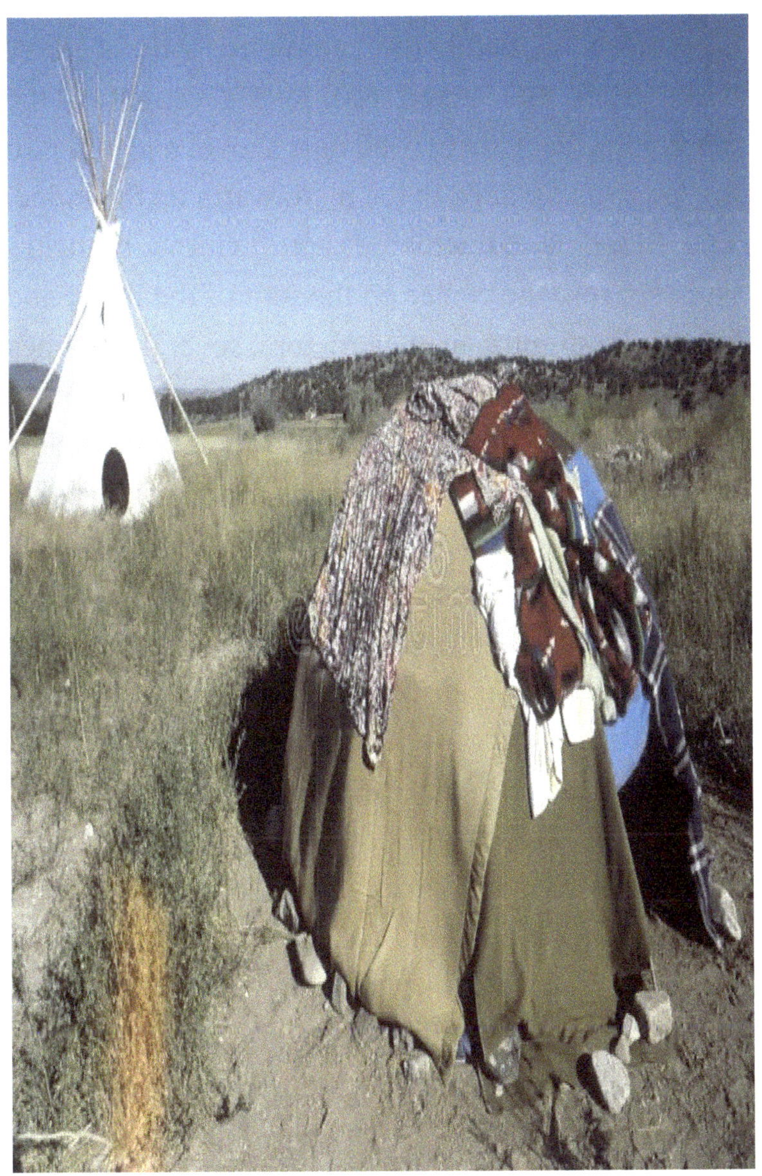

This mound is known as an altar where participants can lay anything special to them.

Before we begin the ceremony, four hot lava rocks from the sacred fire in the center of the medicine wheel are carried on a shovel and slid into the lodge and placed in the pit to warm up the lodge. The lodge is constructed with willow branches gathered into the center on the roof of the lodge and bound. To strengthen the structure, several branches are bound and horizontally woven from the top to the bottom of the lodge. The floor of the lodge, where we would be sitting was covered in cedar bows. The lodge was covered then with blankets and/or canvas in such a way that absolutely no light can be seen from inside the lodge when dark. Nowhere that cold air can seep in...no cracks.

As the darkness falls Women drum and chant, walking in single file to the site. The Women extend a rope from tree to tree for our clothing once we disrobe, as to keep our clothes from getting damp. We form a circle around the fire, taking hands, and we chant. Then it's time to walk over to the clothes line and disrobe, keeping a towel if one wishes, to cover with until inside the lodge or to wipe sweat off during the sweat.

I walk around the inside of the circle marking each woman on her forehead with the Woman symbol.

The women are informed of the password to get into and out of the Lodge, which is "All My Relations" (Mitakuye Oyasin in Lakota). We proceed into the Lodge one at a time, crawling on our hands and knees in a clockwise motion right around the lodge. Once everyone is in and seated with legs crossed in the lotus position we begin. When the flap for the door is closed you will be shoulder to shoulder but won't be able to see one another. The keeper of the door stands guard outside the doorway, and will be ready to open the flap should someone wish to leave between the four rounds. She also tends to anyone that felt the heat was too much and left the lodge. The leader may ask for four more rocks to begin, to warm up the lodge again. Once the four rocks are retrieved from the fire and slid over to the doorway, the keeper of the door will open the flap, and the rocks will be slid into the center pit. I would then welcome the Grandfathers (rocks) and sprinkle water on the red hot rocks to create steam, and then the first round begins. The first round is a prayer for Mother Earth. Once the first woman says her prayer out loud, she will say "next" so others know she is finished her prayer. Then I would sprinkle more water on the hot rocks to create more steam. After each woman has had her turn I sprinkle water on the rocks, and by now everyone is feeling the heat. More rocks from the fire are requested...the flap opens and all our prayers in the form of steam are released to go upwards to the Creator. The new hot rocks are slid in and the flap quickly closes. The second round is a prayer for someone else that was made aware before the weekend began that you would be bringing them into the lodge in spirit. One at a time each woman would pray and say "next" when through, and more water is sprinkled on the rocks creating more and more steam. By this time no one is dilly dallying and say 'next' quickly when finished. By now you are breathing in heat and connecting with the heat by visualizing cords coming from you and attaching to the hot rocks, becoming one with the heat. I will be passing water around the circle constantly for anyone to drink, or dump over their heads. The sweat is pouring off you by now, like you are standing under a shower head. The second round's prayers are released when the flap opens and more rocks come in. The third round is a prayer for yourself. Everyone speaks, and the steam builds.

The fourth round is a Give Away round...letting you give away something about yourself that has served you well but you are now ready to give away. Some women give away excess weight, or their sarcasm, anger, or cigarettes, whatever it is, they release it to spirit. The heat grows with the stream. When the fourth round is over the flap is opened and the steam once again rises to the heavens. Women begin to crawl out of the lodge using the password. The steam rising off their naked bodies...and they just lay on the grass for a while, or, when there is a small stream beside the lodge they get in and lay down. When ready, they go to the clothes line and get dressed. Then everyone solemnly walks to where the feast is being served. The sharing begins, and the hugs abound. After the feast everyone retires for the night.

Application

Choosing the Sweat Lodge card indicates to you that a deep cleansing of energies picked up along your entire life's journey, your lived/learned conditioning, whether in a sauna, or in a Sweat Lodge, is vital now. Cleansing to your very core, the heat opening you up more and more to speak from your heart and listen from your heart. For you to manifest all that you desire your entire being needs to be clear and open. There is no time like the present.

The Earth is our Mother, we must take care of her,
The Earth is our Mother, we must take care of her,
Unite my people, be One,
Unite my people, be One.

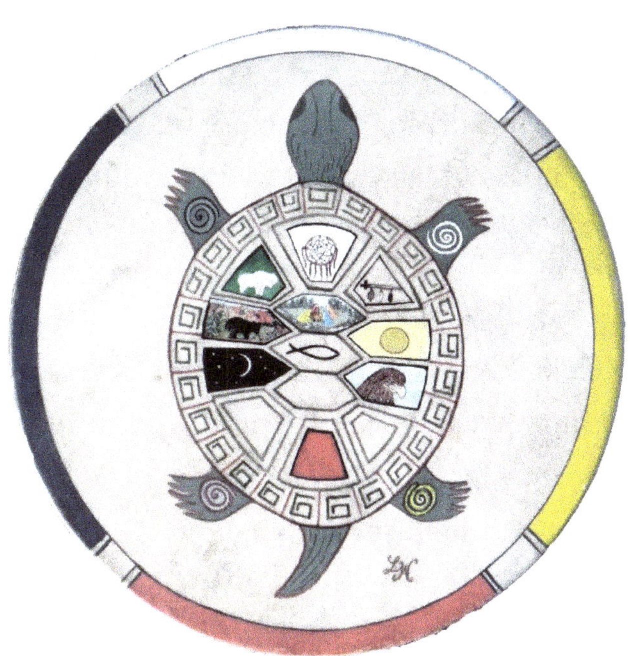

8. Collective Energy

In all of my Healing Circles, and among all my colleagues and friends, you will often hear the term – Holding a Vision. When anyone isn't well, or having difficulties of some kind, and even at times of Joy in one's life, we hold a vision, a sort of prayer together on behalf of anyone that needs especially powerful energy sent and retained/held collectively on their behalf, for as long as it takes to manifest. An example in the case of illness...within our group we will agree to hold a vision collectively...each and every time we think of that person, we would see he or she well again, healed, and beyond that illness.

Collective energy is a powerful tool. One of our Drumming Circle participants was waiting for a liver transplant, and our Drumming Circle, and our church faith family, including our church women's group, and everyone we all knew, held a vision together of Cindy actually well again, having received her transplant. It was a long haul sure enough. In fact at one point, after three years of waiting for that call, we wondered in our hearts if she was even well enough to receive a transplant for she failed so much...but we held our vision just the same.

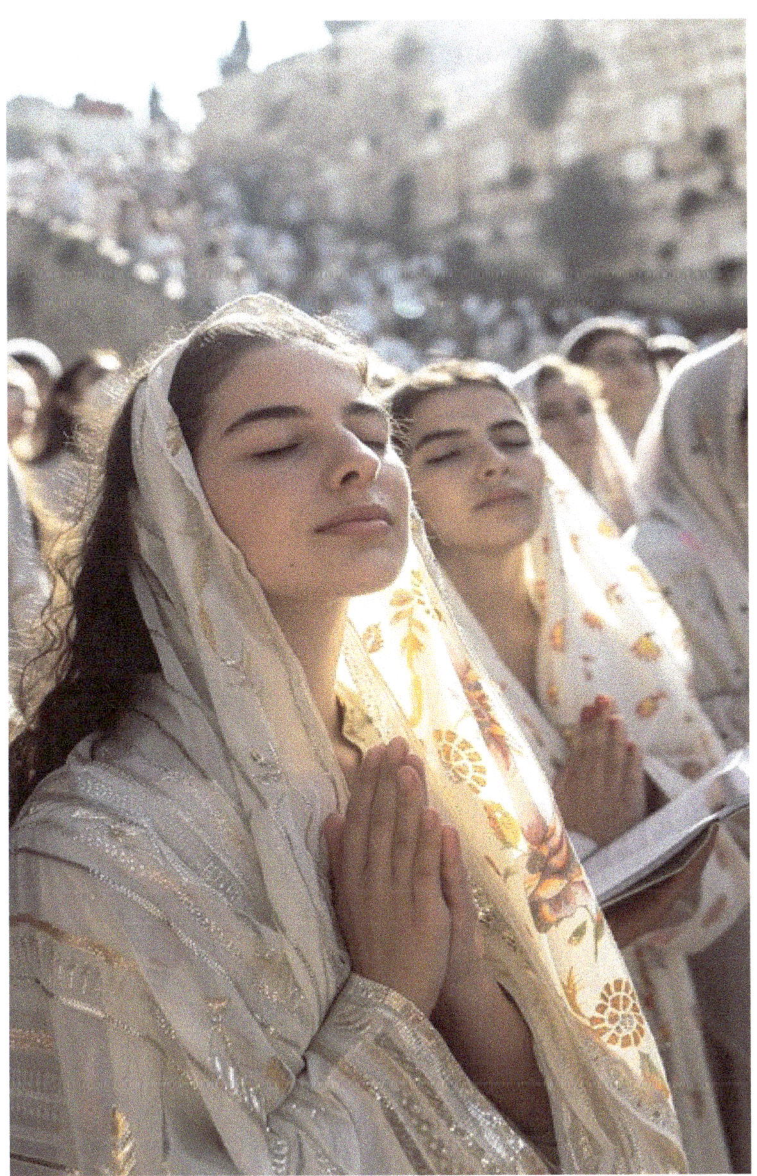

She had two calls in a row to come in and be prepped for the surgery, and they both turned out to be livers that weren't good. But we all continued to hold that vision with her just the same. Finally, she got the third call to be at the hospital at a certain time and be prepped for surgery. This time the liver was acceptable, and Cindy received a new liver. Today she is the vision of wellness, gaining the weight back that she had lost, eating well once again, smiling and ever so grateful to the person that she received her liver from and his or her family, and exceedingly grateful for all those that held that collective vision with, and for her.

This phenomenon of collective human consciousness is real, and when you see it come to life exactly as visioned it seems like magic, and in essence, it really is.

Praise be to Spirit!!!

We are One in the Spirit
We are One in the World,
We are One in the Spirit
We are One in the World,
And we pray that all Unity
Will one day be restored,

And we know we are Sisters by our Love, by our Love,
And we know we are Sisters by our Love.

Application

If the matter that is on your mind and your heart feels like it needs more than only your prayers alone, don't be shy to reach out to all those that are of like mind and heart in your world, to Hold a Vision with you collectively. Whether they are near, or far from you, this is the most powerful thing you can do, especially when you wonder how you can help this along, or help at all.

As a matter of fact we are more powerful than you can imagine. Surprisingly more powerful. I would go so far as to say that Collective energy is taking the matter to a higher universal frequency and allowing us all to see, and know, Unity as well.

French philosopher Pierre Teilhard de Chardin even once said that "We are not human beings having a spiritual experience. We are spiritual beings having a human experience."

May It Be So

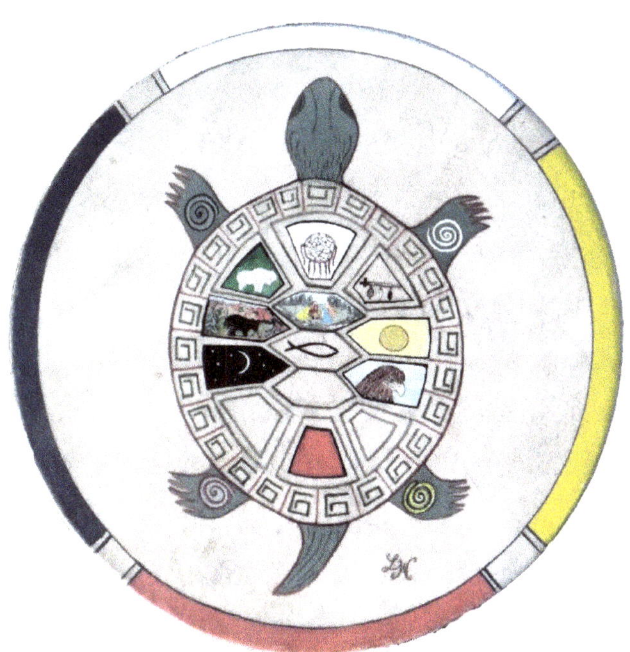

9. Turtle

To say that Turtle played 'a role' in the Native Creation Story is an understatement. In fact, when Sky Woman walked the circumference of the Turtle's shell with a small amount of soil from the ocean floor, her shell grew to the size of North America, better known in the Native community as Turtle Island, according to legend.

When observing the Turtle's back, we see that the outer rim has twenty-eight squares, reflecting the cycle of Grandmother Moon, and of Women, and in the middle of Turtle's shell are thirteen sections, symbolic of the thirteen Moons in a year. Her design for many millennia has spoken of her sacred place in current and in ancient history.

As the oldest symbol for Planet Earth, we are asked by Turtle to be mindful of the cycle of give and take, to give back to Mother Earth as she has given to us. Turtle's teachings are to take it slow and easy, to ensure your safe arrival to your destination.

Turtle medicine is most sacred in my world, and that is reflected in the picture on the back of each of my Tarot Cards in this deck. Blessed Be.

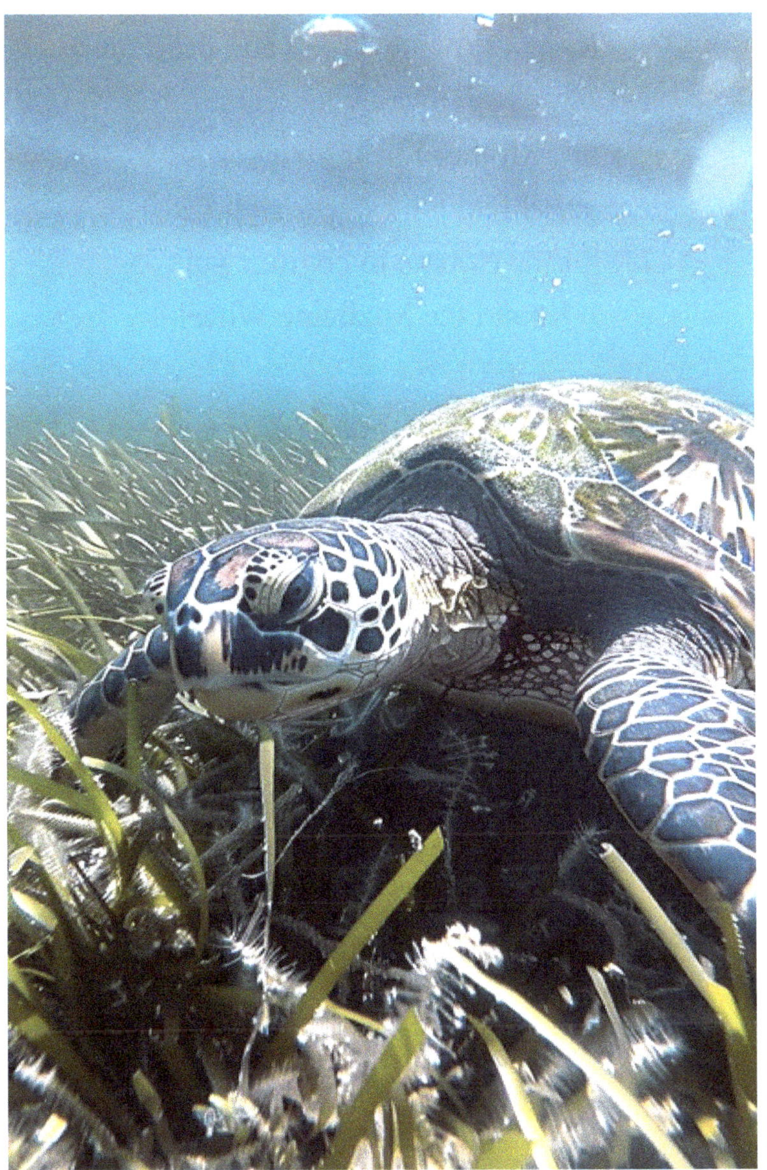

I walk your sacred ground,
Healing waters I have found,
Rivers flowing strong and deep
Wash away your tears.
Mother I hear your cry,
I feel your every sigh,
I have come to comfort you
Round the Medicine Wheel

Application

If Turtle has graced your reading today, you are being put on notice to slow down.

To connect with the Creator and take a moment to celebrate who you were, and who you are created to be. You learn in life that if you 'haven't got time' to slow down, our blessed bodies will slow us down. Whether that be in sickness or in a stark revelation.

Turtle medicine teaches that when we take from the Earth, it is vital that you give something back. When walking in the woods, if, for example, it is a wild herb that's needed for medicine, I will remove the part of the plant that I seek for medicinal purposes, and plant oats or grain near by to give back in thanks to Mother Earth. The Earth's bounty isn't for raping...it is a gift, there for your well being. In fact, even in your own yard, if a certain wild herb is there, it's only there because you need it. Only take what you need, and only 1/3 of the plant, leaving the rest for the next 7 generations, as our Aboriginal people have been instructed, by their ancestors.

Take a walk, have a nap in Nature...pray for the healing you need, and listen to the advise given. Slow and easy always wins the race.

10. Breathe

When I attended Yoga classes I learned that the breath aspect of yoga is known as pranayama in Sanskrit. (Breath) Prana means life force, while ayama means stretching. Breathing deeply through your nose and out through your mouth, extending the breaths in and the breaths out, calms the mind, and the physical postures help you focus on your breath.

Even while gardening, I found that when I stretched and inhaled deeply oxygen was going to my muscles, and the next day I wasn't stiff and sore as a result. Exactly what I was doing in yoga class, breathing deeply when going into the stretches.

In all cases when focusing on your breaths in and breaths out, extending the length of both I can bring my blood pressure from 170 (top number) to 124 in five minutes (in the dental surgeon's chair). Remarkable.

The speed at which you breathe dictates how long you will live. If you breathe fifteen times per minute you will live to 70 or 80 years. If you breathe through your mouth, extending the length of the breaths in and the breaths out ten times per minute you will live to 100.

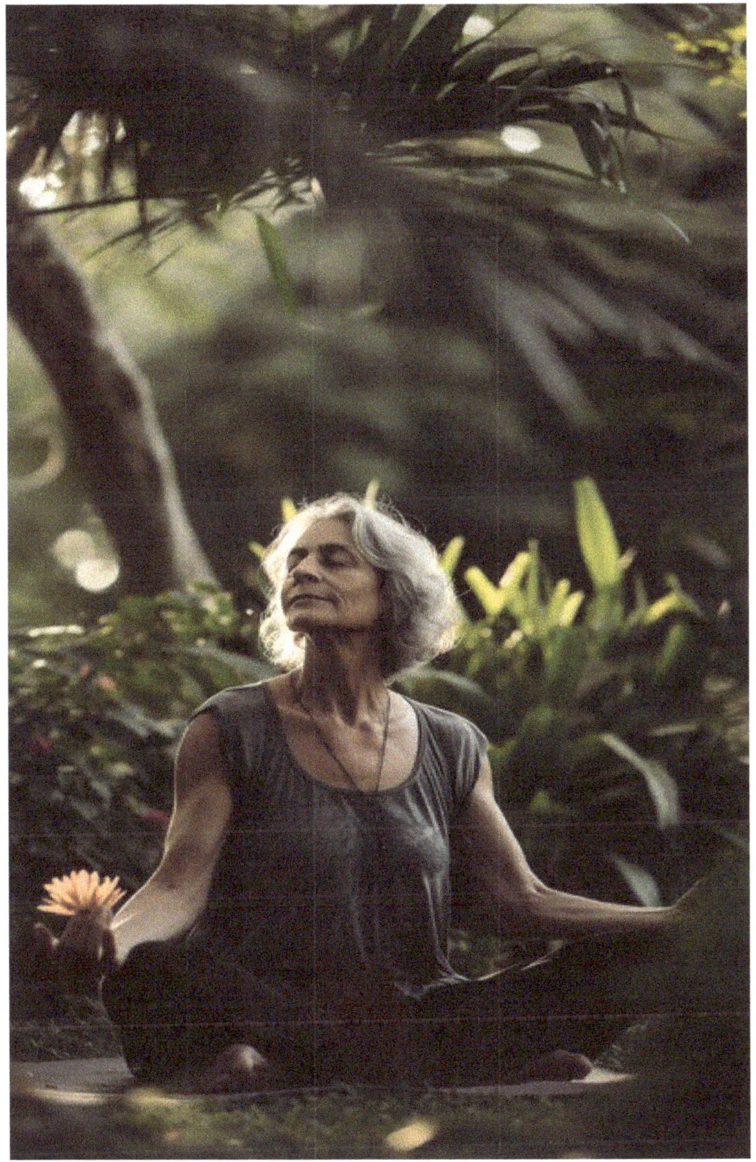

Once again....Breathe deeply, Breathe deeply, in through your nose, out in through.

Breathing consciously has a biological effect on our mental, emotional, and physical state. Blessed Be.

Application

When you choose the Breathe card in a reading it indicates that those times when you are extremely stressed and you find yourself holding your breath, it's time to learn how to breathe, and to remove yourself from the situations that stress you to that extent.

Joining a Yoga class would present one way to learn about breathing deeply, consciously. Breathing consciously can be done anywhere. In the grocery store, in the bathtub, in a meeting, absolutely anywhere. Being in Nature is my go to. Walking in the woods, communing with all things in the wild, from butterflies to trees and moss. Being near the shoreline and balancing one's breathing works for me too.

You are being called to follow guidelines that are presented in meditation, and in Nature or, by and Elder and of course when you consult self in a reading. Know where it is you need to be to balance your being and take the responsibility to do so. May It Be So.

11. Drum

The first Drum was made by Sky Woman and her Daughter, by stretching a deer hide over a stump, and using an antler for a striker. The beat of the Drum is considered by North American Native People to be the heartbeat of Mother Earth. Remember, the first sound we heard was in the womb...the heartbeat of our Mother.

I attended a Workshop with Brooke Medicine Eagle, a Lakota Sioux First Nations Woman, living in rural Montana. The seven foot round Drum in the middle of the Circle had as many as eight Women drumming the heartbeat together all weekend long. When someone's arm got tired, she would raise her other arm, and someone would come and replace her. When Brooke picked up her own drum and started drumming a chant, the center drum picked up the beat joining in. When the beating of Brooke's drum was a quicker beat than the heartbeat, you could feel your heart, that had been beating along with the heartbeat, quicken, often feeling like our hearts were going to jump out of our chests. There were 250 attendees at that workshop. It was fabulous...something I'll never forget.

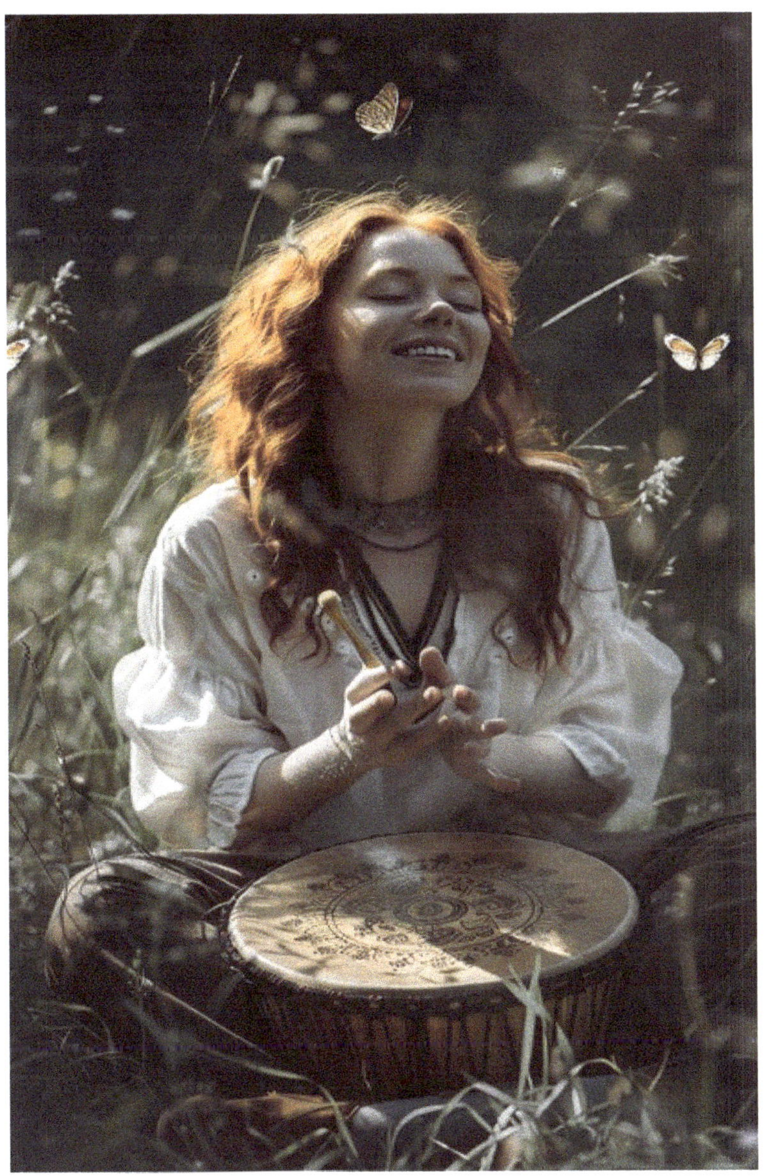

I recall a drumming that I attended in the woods, near Walton Nova Scotia. The drumming was a celebration for the Autumn Equinox's arrival and we played without any breaks in the drumming, for four hours straight.

It felt like we were playing in accelerated time, for the four hours were over in what seemed, no time.

No one spoke, no one chanted....we just drummed together. It really was quite magical.

Our drums are round, like our Mother Earth, Grandmother Moon and Grandfather Sun. Like the Moon Lodge, Medicine Wheel, and the Sweat Lodge. We Circle for this reason, and when in a Circle no one is in front of you, or behind you. You can see the face of everyone there.

A Shamanic drumming generally entails Shamanic journeying, and the Drum is the lifeline guiding the journeyer back to ordinary reality. Blessed Be.

Application

As the heartbeat of Mother Earth the drum is the pulse of life and the primal rhythm. The Drum tells us to get in touch with our feelings. People use the drum to open the heart and bring healing. The drum presents a quality of sound heard in the voices of people that speak from their heart.

It could be time to find or make a drum for yourself, and match your being with the rhythm of Mother Earth. Your heart will open, and bring the healing you seek, to you.

Something that you have held silently in your heart needs to be set free. There really is no better way to do this than by drumming. You will feel its rhythmic flow and experience a trance like state, grounding you. Everyone and everything in the light of your love will benefit from your healing.

May It Be So.

12. Moon Lodge

For each of the thirteen Moons in a calendar year, when the Moon was only a slight slit in the Western night's sky, the Women, the Crones of the Tribe, left the camp taking the children and the Mothers with them so that the bleeders could bleed together for the next three days. (Three days....not ten...not filled with cramps.) They didn't hold it back subconsciously believing that this was a curse. These women weren't taught that their monthly periods were a curse...they were taught that it is a life giving gift. During their time in the Moon Lodge the visions of the Women were shared, while the gravity of the Moon pulled their blood from them, out, and into the Cedar bow flooring below them, into the Earth....as a gifting back to Mother Earth for her Bounty. They prayed and drummed and sang. The Crones listened and taught the way of the ancestors, and attained all of their Wisdom as well. While they attended the Moon Lodge the men were in the Sweat Lodge, praying.

If a girl received this life-giving gift at, for example, age eleven, by the time she was sixteen she had already attended sixty-five Moon Lodges.

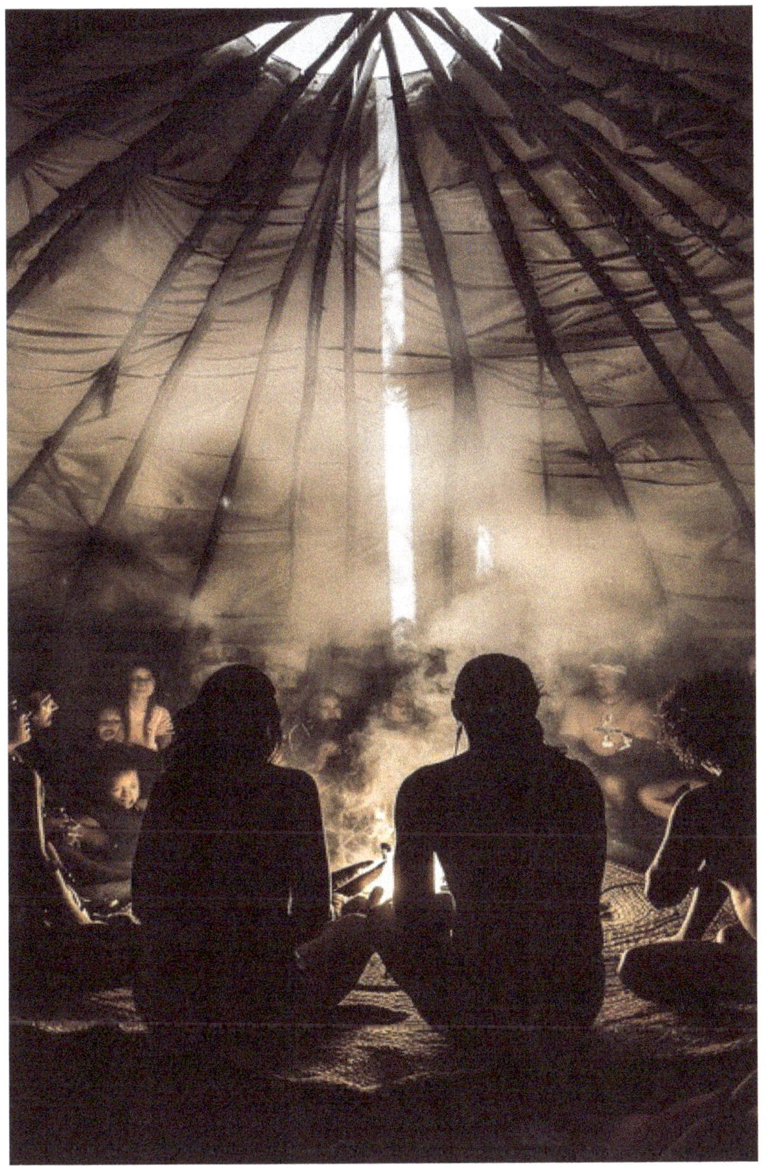

A Crone that is seventy years old, has attended 910 Moon Lodges...The Crone holds sway in the tribe for good reason, for she has gained the most Wisdom. When the three days pass by, the Women returned to find the men waiting, eagerly, to hear the Wisdom and the Visions received by the Women.

Visions such as, which long house to live in, what to hunt next for food and for medicine, where to move the camp next. They didn't over fish, or over grow.. over take...there was no raping of the Earth. Always giving back. Always improving the space they'd be moving from. When something was taken from the Earth, likewise something was gifted back to the Mother...Life was much different then, before colonization. The North American Native peoples' Spirituality is something they live each and every day of their lives. Unlike Christianity, this way of knowing was all that life consisted of everything was based on Spirituality every day following the stars, and the seasons of the Medicine Wheel of Life.

I give away this Blood of life to All My Relations,
And I open my womb to the light.
I give away this Blood of life to All My Relations,
And I open my womb to the light.
Give away, give away, give away, give away,
I open my womb to the light.

Application

When this powerful teaching comes to you in a reading, your life is about to deepen in every way. Your focus for this reading and all that you have wondered about or questioned is about to be answered. The answers will come within your own innate wisdom. The imprints in your DNA that belonged to your ancestors is opening up, or exposing itself to you now. Your intuition will astound, and your reserve will strengthen.

All that is required from you is to watch, and to listen. Be especially mindful of what appears to be random happenings, visits, and from Nature's many ways to grab your attention. The rustling of the leaves in applause for you. Or a butterfly happening by, or perhaps a bird's song will catch your attention. You don't ask for these signs to appear, as much as, they appear whenever you need them. They always have. The things you learn as you grow will feel more like remembering(s) to you, rather than new information. Trust.

13. Gifting Ceremony

As a rule, I would end my workshop weekends with a Gifting Ceremony. Prior to the weekend I asked the attendees to bring something that they may find in their closets, drawers, cedar chests, or jewelry boxes...that they have kept for a long time for various reasons. Often they kept things that they never used or wouldn't purchase for themselves. Most often it might be something that was very important at one time in their lives, and held sentiment, but in some way or another has lost its meaning over time, whether because of a relationship ending or some other reason. I asked them to bring the item to the workshop weekend, unwrapped, to give away in a gifting ceremony.

When they arrived on the Friday night they picked a name out of a hat and were asked to shadow that person unknowingly, for the weekend. To observe her grace, her beauty within, the way she moved and spoke...everything lovely about her.

On the last day of the workshop, as our last ceremony for our time together, I placed a wicker tray in the center of the Circle, and the Women placed the items they brought to give away on the tray.

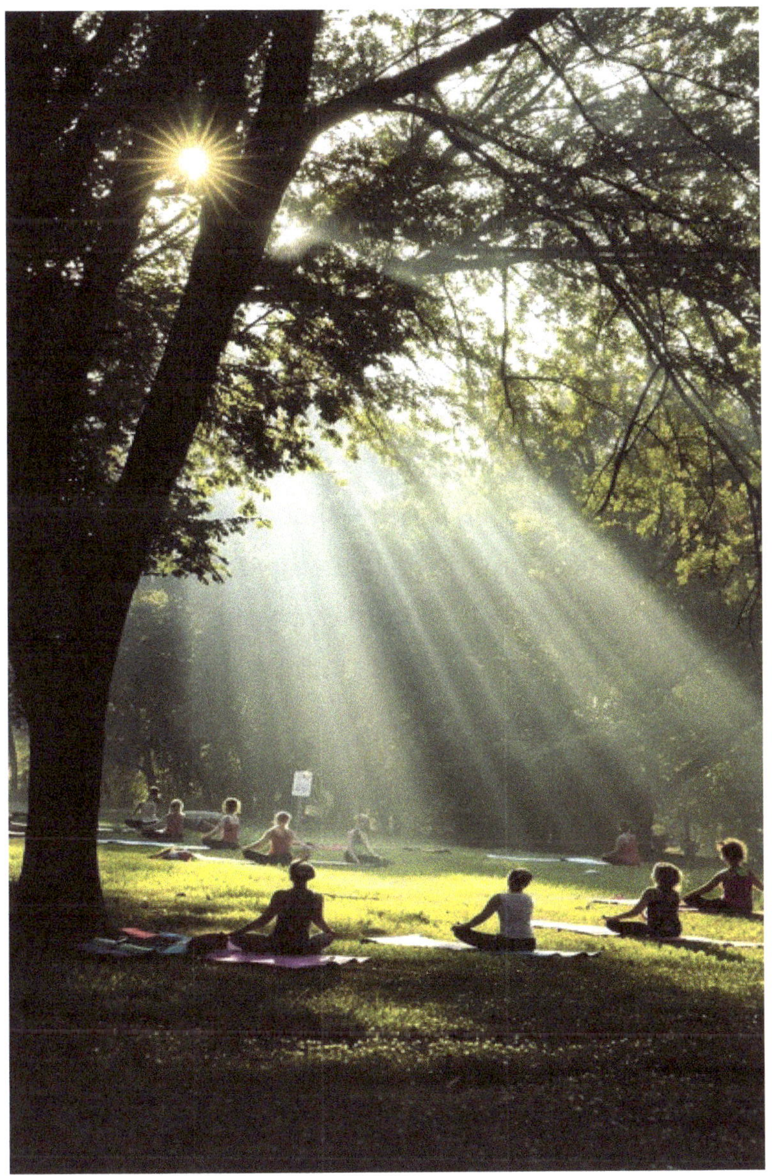

As the ceremony began, the person on my left would look into the eyes of the Woman she shadowed all weekend and begin telling her the beautiful attributes she noticed about her.

This part of the ceremony was especially moving. Quite often there were tears shed by both women. Following this, the Woman that was shadowed would choose something off the tray in the center of the Circle. Then, she would look into the eyes of the Woman she shadowed and speak to her of her attributes. Once again, when everything had been expressed to the shadowed Woman she would choose something from the tray that drew her. This process continued until everyone had a gift and everyone had been gifted with all the beauty that someone else saw in her.

We would go around the Circle once again and tell what we brought to the ceremony, and why we kept it until now, and why they felt it was time to part with the item. Following that, we went around the Circle for the last time and explained what drew her to the item she chose. It was all a very beautifully moving experience.

It was magical listening to the reasons Women were ready to let go of an item, and to the reasons that they were drawn to a certain item off the tray. Everything correlated, making this an incredibly special time together.

Application

Going through the process of choosing an item to finally let go of, after keeping it, for a reason over the years, is an exercise in growth in one's life. Of letting go. This card is a challenge for you to do the same, but only when you are ready. Experiencing another person choosing that gift is comforting, just knowing that the item will have a good home, was chosen for a reason, and will serve the Woman (that you shadowed), well.

The Gifting Ceremony card has dropped into your reading for a reason. Only you know what that reason could be. Perhaps the next time there is a gathering you will suggest this ceremony to them, bringing warmth and growth to all that attend.

In all cases, this card assures that there are various ways to bring warmth and growth to anyone, anytime. So is the way of gifting, and of receiving, meaningfully.

Namaste'. The Divine in Me Bows to The Divine in You.

There is a Woman that Weaves the Night Sky,
See her Spin, watch her Fingers Fly
She is Within Us, Beginning to End
Our Grandmother, our Sister, our Friend.

She is the Weaver, and We are the Web,
She is the Needle, and We are the Thread.
She Changes everything she Touches,
And everything she Touches Changes.

14. Womb of the Universe

Ilarion Merculleff, Deputy Director Alaska Native Science Commission teaching shared by Agi, a Shaman, Eldest on St. Paul Island. Ilarion explains...He told me to go to the ocean, 'quieten your mind, center yourself, and set your intention, and the answers will come'….

I tapped into the womb at the Center of the Universe.

This is where we get our information.

Our Ceremony, our Guidance, our Direction comes from that place that put new meaning to the statement "All things are birthed of Woman."

All Creativity and All Creation.

I touched into, what might be called the Sacred Feminine.

And that was profound for me…it changed my life, just to see that.

And, this is also why Women were considered sacred. This is a very important point, especially today.

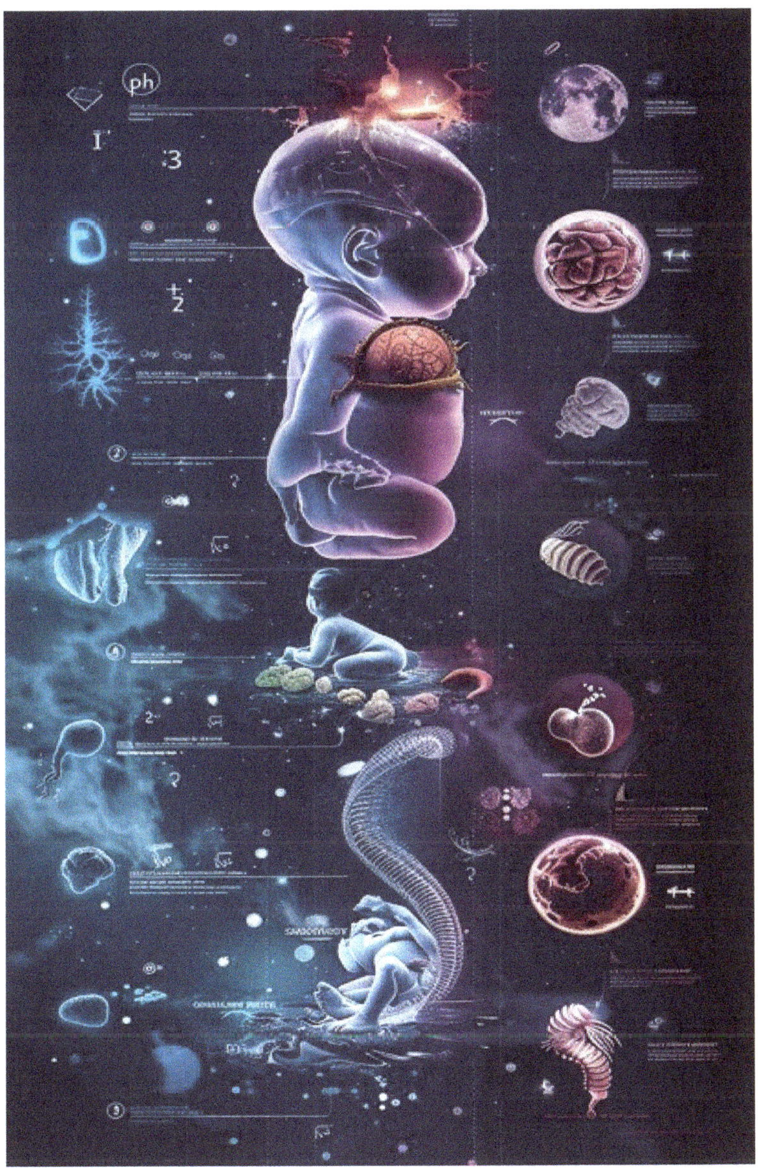

Most men and women, and even some religious leaders, have forgotten why women were considered sacred. Because like a hologram inside of their body, there's the direct, and the exact sacred condition as the womb in the center of the Universe, that is physically manifested in their womb.

Now, western medicine would say 'well you know, we can take the egg and the sperm outside of the womb and we can, start life', but it can never grow into a human being, and the scientists can't understand why. From a traditional way we understand there is a sacred vibrational field inside of the woman that we have forgotten to honor, that is the place of all the things born, that nothing can be birthed without Woman, and what women have done before time began, is that they would take that sacred vibration and move it outside in ceremonial space to create the womb on the outside vibrationally, so that something new can be birthed in this world. And we've forgotten that point. And its really, really important now.

The men, have to be the new spiritual warriors, ones that protect the sacred space of women so they can do their work. Because if we are looking for change in this world, from a spiritual standpoint, and from a physical stand point, it will never happen until we restore that place.

Until we help women do that. Nothing new will be created, and so if we don't do it, I believe we as a human species are done for.

There is a secret one inside
All the stars and all the galaxies
Run through her hands like beads.

Application:

Your Ancestors are calling you, praying you will re-member them, their way of life, the spiritual ways they lived WITH daily; Lived with the Earth, the Sun, and the Moon, and All Our Relations as One. This, and so much more, will help you to navigate your way through the dynamic before you. The secret one inside knows, re-members.

When you Meditate, tap into those that have gone before you, arriving in you, and those you pass along for the next seven generations...from the Original Mother on down. Be with them, look into their eyes and find all the teachings you need for this lifetime and for your seed trail. We create our own reality with every breath we take and every thought we think. Your answers are with your ancestor's and when you receive the teachings you will know them not as new information. But as re-memberings. Blessed Be.

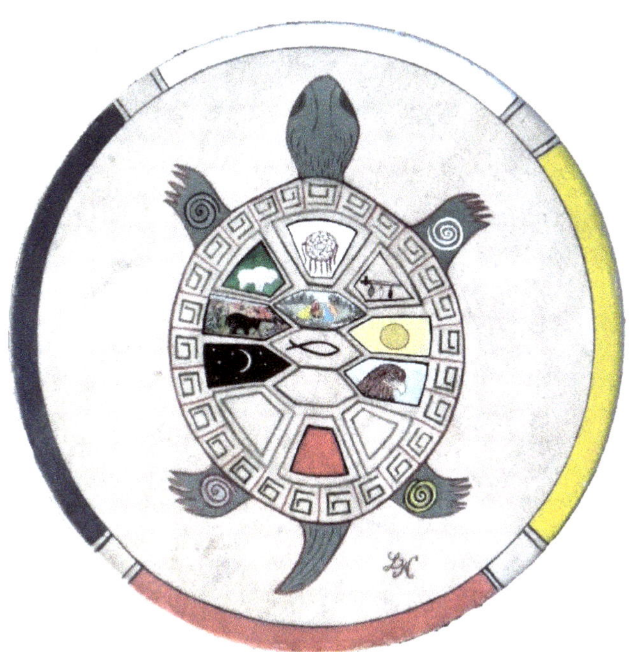

15. Sky Woman

This Creation story is of the First Nations people of Turtle Island (North America).

Long before our Earth was created lived a Woman in another world with her husband and a community of tribal people. This Woman is known as Sky Woman, and she was a very inquisitive person. She was also pregnant. She was always asking why? When? Who? Where? One day she asked her husband, the keeper of the Tree of Life, just exactly was under the tree. He didn't know. Other than roots in the soil, he had no idea. Sky Woman continued to plead with him to uproot the tree so she could see what was under it. Finally, her husband couldn't take it any longer, and he uprooted the tree as she wished. Of course, there was a huge hole under the roots of that tree. Sky Woman looked down the hole and bent over as far as she could to be able to see what was under there. She bent over so far, that she fell...and as she fell, she tried to brace her fall by grabbing plants and roots, but ended up with them in her hand, and she continued to tumble and fall, for what seemed to be

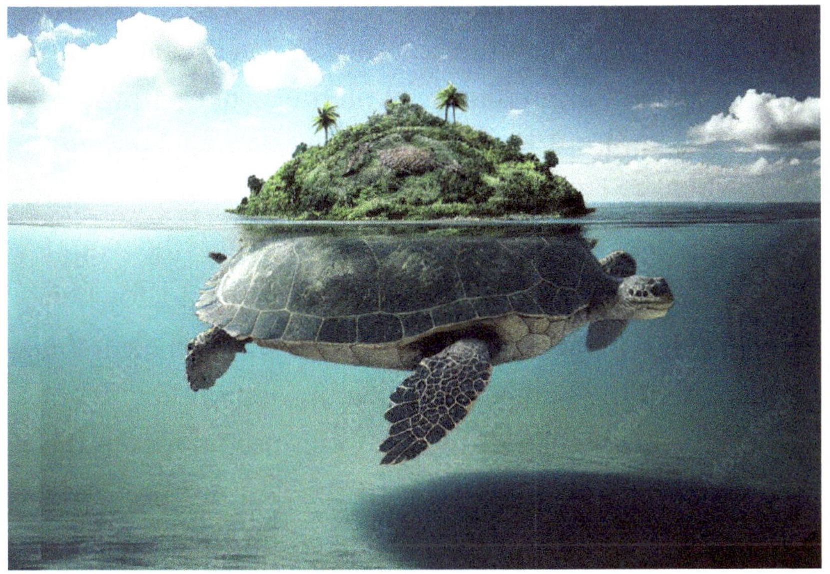

an eternity. The roots she had in her hands were roots of the strawberry, of corn and tobacco.

Sky Woman tumbled and continued to fall seeing nothing but sky.

The waterfowl noticed her falling and flew under her attempting to brace her fall and lower her gently. Asking permission of the sea turtle to allow them to lower her onto his back, he agreed. Once they lowered her onto the turtle's back, she began to complain immediately, which was her nature.

She said, "Where I come from there is land, not just water...where is the land?"

Attempting to satisfy her curiosity the water fowl tried to dive and look for some land for her. Many of them knew that there was soil on the bottom of the ocean, but when they attempted to get to the bottom they drowned. Otter tried to get to the bottom to grab a paw full of the soil on the ocean floor. He made several attempts until finally he did reach the bottom and was able to grab some soil there. He swam back to the surface, very much out of breath, and he handed the soil to Sky Woman. She began walking counterclockwise around the surface of the turtle's back, and as she did, the surface became larger and larger. She kept walking and eventually she created North America or Turtle Island, as we know it today. She planted the roots she brought with her, and they grew, providing her with strawberries, corn for further sustenance, and tobacco for ceremony. This land she roamed free, exploring the abundant forests and animals there.

Attempting to satisfy her curiosity the water fowl tried to dive and look for some land for her. Many of them knew that there was soil on the bottom of the ocean, but when they attempted to get to the bottom they drowned. Otter tried to get to the bottom to grab a paw full of the soil on the ocean floor. He made several attempts until finally he did reach the bottom and was able to grab some soil there. He swam back to the surface, very much out of breath, and he handed the soil to Sky Woman. She began walking counterclockwise around the surface of the turtle's back, and as she did, the surface became larger and larger. She kept walking and eventually she created North America or Turtle Island, as we know it today. She planted the roots she brought with her, and they grew, providing her with strawberries, corn for further sustenance, and tobacco for ceremony.

In this land she roamed free, exploring the abundant forests and animals there. She observed the animals giving birth and then consuming the after birth, seemingly to detour predators from realizing there was a helpless baby there. She learned what to do when her own baby, her first, was born. It wasn't long before that day came, and Sky Woman birthed a Daughter. She and her child roamed the land together gathering berries and other edible and medicinal plants. When her Daughter became of age, one night the young woman had a dream. A man came to her in her dream and placed two arrows on her torso. When Sky Woman saw this in the morning she then knew that her Daughter was with child. Once the usual length of time passed her Daughter birthed twin boys. When the twins came, one came the usual way and the other burst out through her side, killing her. It was then up to their Grandmother to raise them. It was said that these twins would quarrel, even in the womb, and they continued to quarrel outside of the womb. As they roamed the Earth, one would create a rose, and the other would put thorns on the stems. One would create and antelope and the other would create coyote to kill the antelope...it was always a fight with everything they did and created, but at the same time, creating balance.

Their Grandmother called them the Mischievous one and the other was the Good One.

Sky Woman grew old and feeble, and eventually she died. The twins fought over her body because the Good One wanted to bury her body, returning her to the Earth, as was done for their Mother. The Mischievous one wanted to throw her off the edge of the Earth. They tugged and tore at her body, and the Mischievous one ended up ripping her head off. Then he flung her head away up into the sky, and she became known as Grandmother Moon just as we know her today. The light of the night's sky. The Good One buried the rest of her body as he wanted to in the first place. He burned tobacco and prayed in ceremony as his Grandmother had taught him. And so is the story of Sky Woman.

Application

If Sky Woman has fallen into your reading today, she comes with many stories of self sustenance. Of learning from nature and all the teachings there, of Medicines and the ways and ceremonies, of tribal ancestors from whence she came. She teaches that climate justice is racial justice. She teaches how the animals on the Earth she created gave her permission to take their bodies, to nourish their bodies and their skins to keep them warm. How she and her Daughter created the first Drum together by stretching a hide across a hollow stump, and play the drum in ceremony. She is also a figure of fertility who provided the first corn to people.

These teachings are the same teachings that, once our Earth tires of man's destruction and raping of her bounty, our aboriginal brothers and sisters will teach everyone on Earth how to live with our planet. Not against her. Your take away here is to further expand the ways you are now learning, of recycling, reusing, and renewing. To make your way to our beautiful Aboriginal brothers and sisters, with respect to learn humbly, everything you can, to, like them, look after the next seven generations on our Mother the Earth. May It Be So.

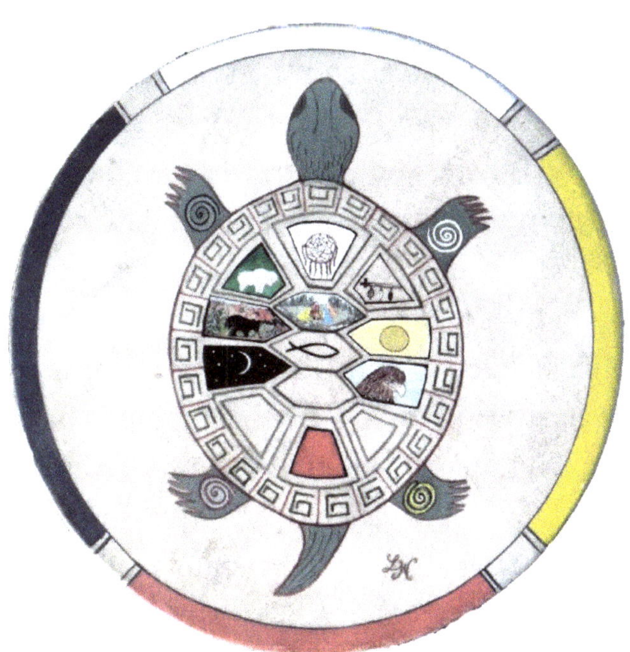

16. Standing People

The Women of our Healing Circle arrived at six o'clock sharp and the hay wagon was hooked up to the John Deere tractor, loaded with hay bales, and was ready to go. Once everyone was loaded on the wagon, we headed to the hay field and all the way down to where the woods started. Once there, I parked the tractor, and everyone disembarked. I explained to everyone that we were going to enter the woods here, and let a tree choose them for a tree ceremony. They were to sit at the base of their tree and close their eyes, and think about a question they would like to ask the tree, known by the First Nation's people as a Standing Person, a question that has been playing on their mind. They stayed there with their Standing Person for as long as they needed to. After about forty-five minutes, once everyone felt they had their answer, they headed back to the Hay Wagon. We got everyone loaded on the wagon and started our journey back to the farmhouse.

No one spoke of their question to their Standing Person, until we had our Chai Tea that was warming on the wood stove.

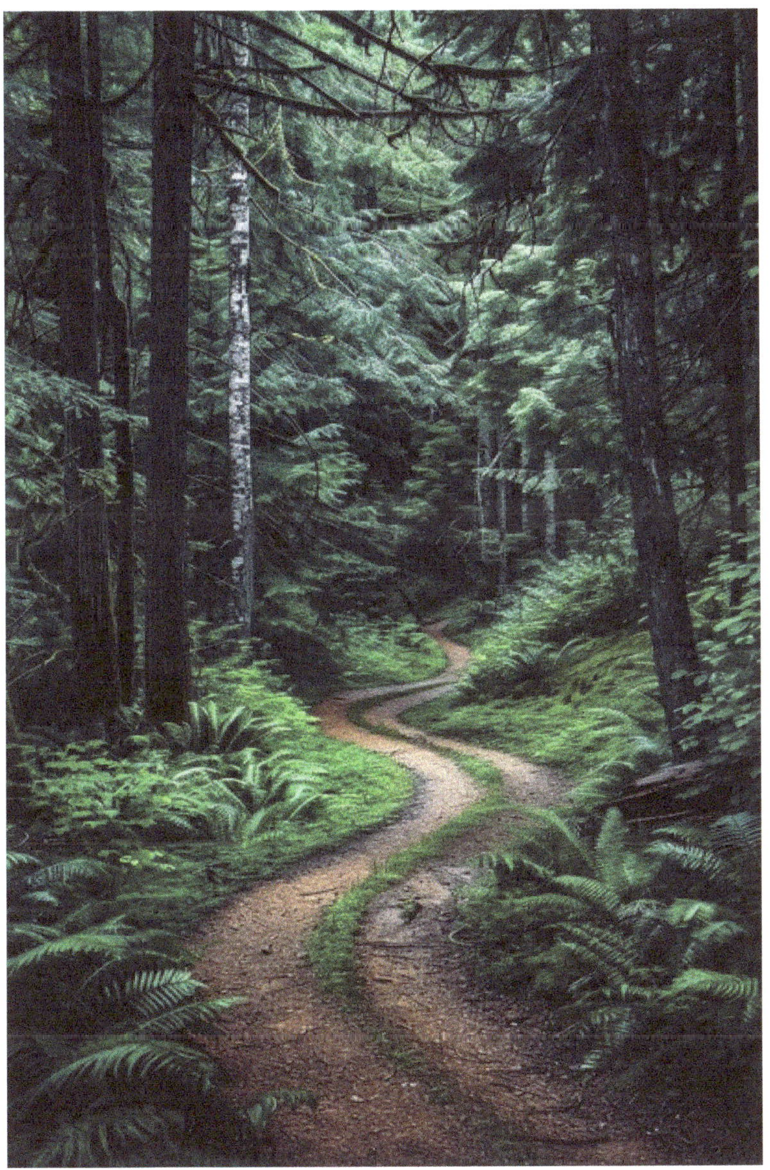

For all our Healing Circles I made Chai Tea and made sure there was lots of Cardamon seeds in the tea. They are believed to assist in opening you up, to speak your words, answering the questions we each proposed to the Standing Person that chose us.

We took our place around the Circle, and we finished our tea, and chanted our gathering song, singing....

Circle me Sisters,
Drink the pure waters,
Let me down softly
Bring me back home.

Beginning on my left, that Woman picked up the Talking Stick and began to share the question that she had for her Standing Person, followed by the answer that she received from her tree. Some of the Women chose to sit at all four directions with their tree, N, S, E, W, receiving four different viewpoints surrounding her question. When that Woman was finished sharing, she would return the Talking Stick to the center of the Circle once again, and the next Woman would pick it up and share her question and the wisdom she received from her visit with the tree that chose her. It was a beautiful experience for all that attended. In fact, they asked if they could do it again sometime soon, together.

Application

Being with a trusted Healing Circle of Women is one of the most enriching experiences anyone can have. When the need to renew, refill our vessels, having that regular space to return to each Moon cycle is comforting and a much-needed venue for all Women and Men.

When we have pressing questions that seem unanswerable, the place to head to, is our Healing Circle. The space for you is always there, and the support you need is never ending, is always confidential, and always provides just like our Moon. She lights our path wherever we go.

There is an abundant supply of wisdom in Nature, and following that advice is exactly what our Aboriginal people did to originally learn to live on the Earth in a balanced way. Following the Moon cycles, that is exactly what their ancestors did.

Bring your questions to the places you need to refill your vessel, which, we as Women give and give and give from, and often forget that when we feel we haven't anything left to give, this signals our vessel is empty. Like our Grandmother the Moon, we cycle and we renew. Love yourself generously and ask Mother Earth to help you.

17. Shamanic Journeying: Discovering your Power Animal

I asked everyone in the Circle to lie down on the floor with a pillow for their heads and close their eyes. First, I chose and instructed someone I trust to do the drumming for the journey, then I asked everyone in the Circle to lie down on the floor with a pillow for their heads and close their eyes. Then the Drum begins a relatively slow beat, having pre-instructed them as follows: to imagine their favourite water source place, and step into the water. Imagine that in the deepest part of the water you can submerge yourself and actually breathe under water! Start looking for a crevice that you can get through that takes you out of the water and that exposes a tunnel going downward. We are heading to the lower world to find your power animal. Your power animal will be your companion on all your Shamanic Journeys, but first you must establish what your power animal is. On your way down the tunnel, observe the textures and colours in your tunnel. Smell the smells there....feel the sides of your tunnel and explore its beauty. As you move downward in this spiralling tunnel you will begin to see light from the lower world coming closer and closer. Once you are at the end of the tunnel, step into the lower world.

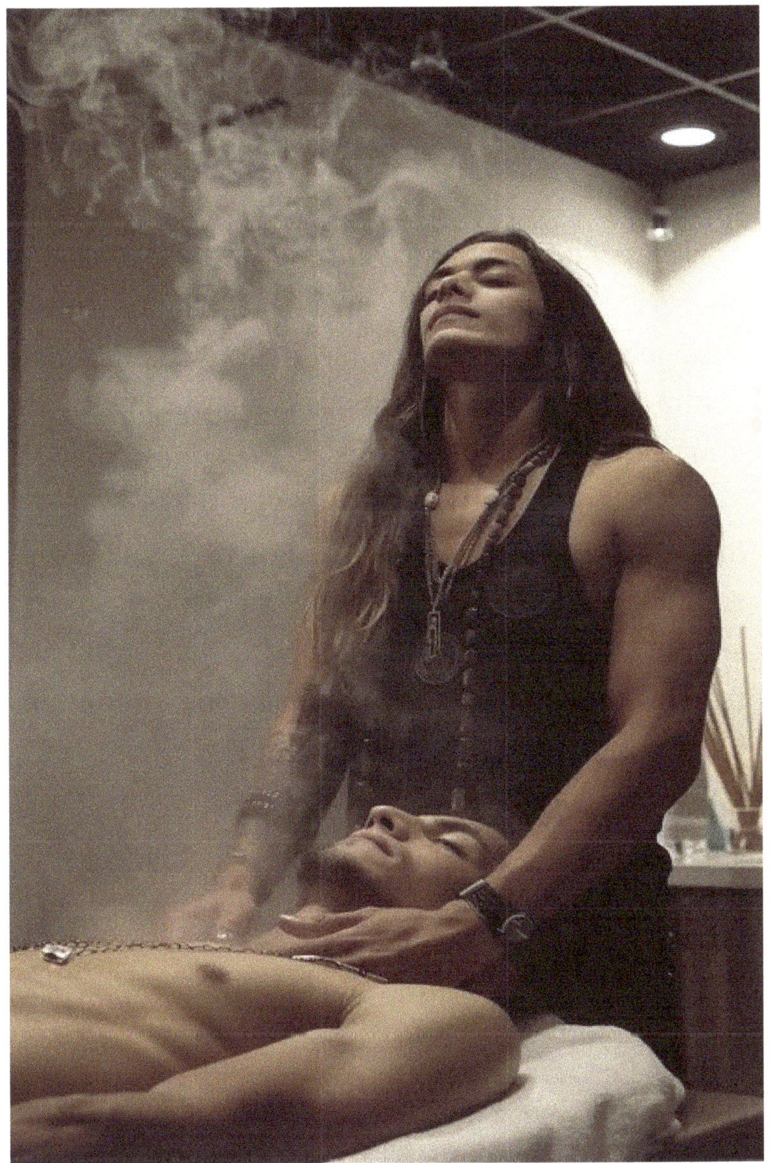

As you look all around you will see a forest of beautiful trees, mosses, and trails... you'll hear sounds like rustling leaves, birds singing, and you'll begin to see critters, one at a time come into your frame of vision. Each one will stop and look your way. Ask, "Are you my power animal?"

If it is not, thank it for coming and see it saunter away. Then another one appears. Again, ask if it is your power animal. Thank it for coming and continue until one appears and answer, "Yes" to your question.

Remember three things; if you see a group of the same animal, such as a herd of deer, this is one sighting. And, if you see a swarm of any insect, simply sidestep the swarm. Lastly, it's not recommended that you play a Shamanic drumming journeying tape CD while driving. Because once you are a seasoned Journeyer you will automatically arrive in the lower world. Your driving won't become erratic however you will likely be driving very fast.

I ask that you affirm that the power animal is yours, once you have seen it in four separate sightings. Once you know for certain that this is your power animal, thank it for coming to you, and still hearing the drumming in the background, take some time to play and frolic with your power animal that will be waiting for you each time you enter the lower world to Journey. Your power animal will accompany you on each and every Journey, whether you are travelling to the upper world where your teachers are, or the middle world of ordinary rcality.

If you travel to the upper world to meet with your teacher, ask your question...listen carefully for the answer, and then prepare to return to the lower world once again. If at any time during your journey you hear your drummer stop drumming, and pause, and then drum rapidly for thirty seconds this is your call home. You must leave where you are and bid farewell to your power animal until you meet again. Tracing you steps back up the tunnel, through the crevice, into the water, then out of the water back into ordinary reality. The drum will stop the rapid beat after the thirty seconds and then you will hear the drum beat seven times...you will hear this four times in a row, signalling that the Journey is over. You will notice that everywhere you go, you will see your power animal in pictures, in person, in books, magazines, online....now that you have acknowledged it, it will be with you always. It always has been with you...but if we ignore our power animals, not knowing what they are....they will leave you. Your power animal will be with you, not in the same way that it is with you on a journey....just in places it has always been but you have never noticed before now.

Application

If Journeying has walked into your reading today, you are asked to acknowledge new ways to have your deepest questions fully answered. One way is Tarot readings, and another is Shamanic Journeying. All that is required here is that you take the time you need to Journey...setting the stage, preparing yourself, and having a drummer, or a good Journeying CD. This is simply one way to nurture and feed yourself as you refill your vessel. We spend almost all our waking hours fulfilling the needs of others, and our vessels empty from time to time. It is up to us, no one else, to know where the places are to go and refill, and to take the time to do so. Otherwise we attempt to function with and empty vessel...and no one benefits from you then, especially yourself.

Learn to schedule time for yourself to refill, to play, to explore new ways to renew and new ways of knowing. Be healthy and wise and ready for anything that comes your way. May it be so....Blessed Be.

18. Herstory

In ancient times, prior to Patriarchy, when the Creator was known as The Goddess, men would marvel at how the Goddess and all Women could bleed every month and yet they didn't die. The men saw this as great power. Power that men wanted...and they believed they could take it from her. After all, they believed they took their penis' from her, so why not this power of bleeding but not dying. The penis, they believed, must have been the Goddess's at one time, because when men stared at the Women's cavity for very long, their penis would react, even from a distance, and it fit right into a Women's cavity. If they could take that from them, surely they could take the power of the blood.

Symbolic of the blood, one man from every village was castrated, and if he lived, he was then named A Priest. (ergo the celibacy that still exists today for Priests of the Roman Catholic Church.) And Patriarch was born. Pope John XXII declared an inquisition on the war on the Nature People (Witches) whose power they feared. The Burning Times began. *9,000,000 European Women died, between AD 600 and 1700 – a period of 1,100 years.

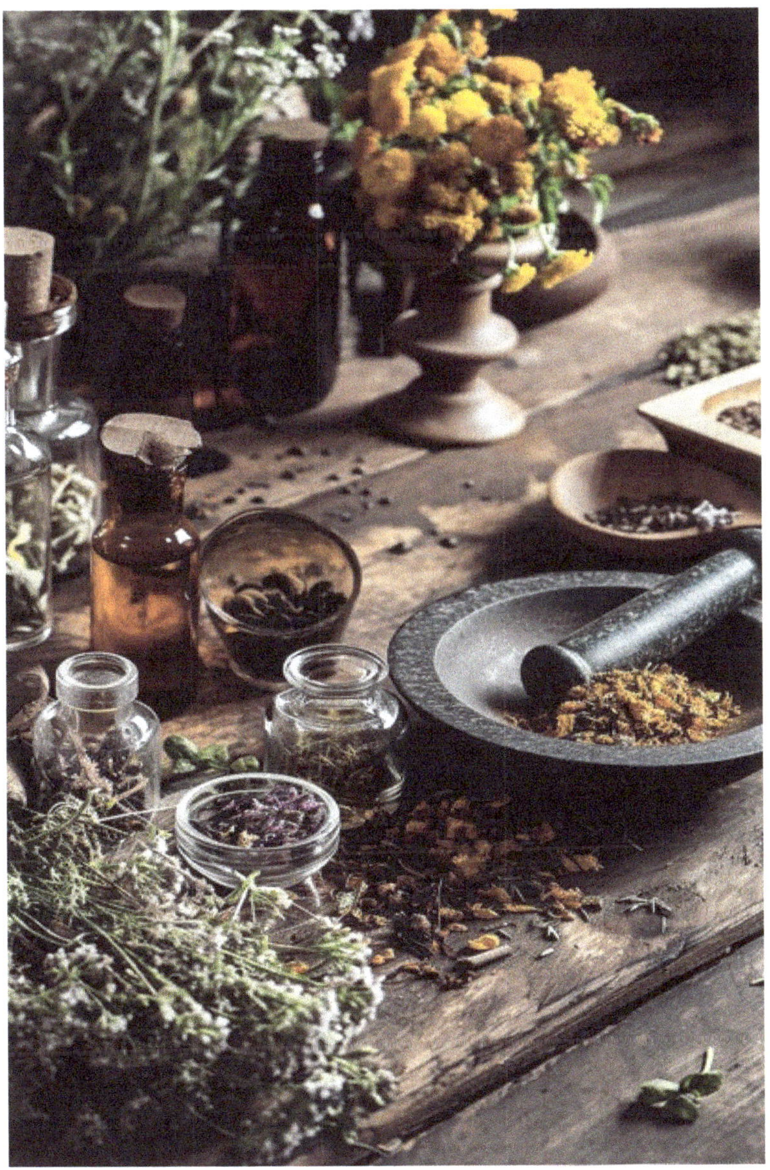

Some burned at the stake as Witches, and some Women chose their death in the sea. They would form a human chain and walk out into the waves together chanting the names of the Goddesses: 'Isis, Astarte, Diana, Hecate, Demeter, Kali, Anna.'

Interestingly, a rule at that time, ONE Woman, convicted of Witchcraft, from each village was spared, and was taken far into the woods to continue her craft. She was to be used as someone for male doctors to consult with, should they ever be stumped with what medicine to offer a patient

References[1]

---

[1] *Women's Rituals, Barbara Walker
* The Burning Times – The National Film Board of Canada. (Check Youtube or your Library)
*a 1784 article by Gottfried Christian Voigy, in which he estimates the figure of 9,442,,994 executions between AD 600 and 1700 – a period of 1,100 years.

Application

Predominantly Women, and some Men were convicted of Witchcraft during the Burning Times. In our time we are open and expressive of our opinions. We can grow our medicines and process them into salves, tinctures, concoctions, etc. Although the pharmaceutical authorities play down anything but their own medicines, at least they aren't declaring another Holocaust over it...yet.

Choosing the Herstory card in a reading demonstrates the hardships the female gender has suffered to come to the place we are now, in History, in Canada,... praises be to the Creatress of all things!

This card signals you to take your place in this freedom 'current'. Nurture and nourish yourself in the ways that Mother Nature has provided for us. Do your research and be sure to carefully study the possible interactions many pharmaceuticals have with herbals. In terms of Women's menopausal remedies for example, Susan Weed is a wonderful resource teacher, for one. Consult your physician as well, and if you are fortunate enough to have an open and informed doctor...you are blessed.

You will find that whatever it is you will benefit from using, in teas, salves, tinctures or any concoctions, will likely be right outside your door. That's why it's there, my dears! Ho!

19. The Medicine Wheel

The Medicine Wheel, from the perspective of North American Native teachings, is a Circle of four colours, honouring the four races of man. In the East, the starting place, where the day and the wheel of the seasons begin, the colour is Yellow. Some of the characteristics in the East are illumination, vision, competitive, enthusiasm, and the Season is Spring. The animal in the East is Hawk or Eagle.

In the South the place of rapid growth, the colour is Red, and the season is Summer. Some of the characteristics of the South are, being detailed, analytical, task oriented, non assertive. The animal in the South is Mouse. In the West, the going within place, like the bear retreating to its den, the colour is Black. Some of the characteristics of the West are, warm, cuddly, attentive, supportive, and the Season is Autumn. The animal in the West is Bear.

In the North the colour is White. Some of the characteristics of the North are driving, assertive, cool, distant, and the season is Winter. The animal in the North is Buffalo.

The Middle of the Medicine Wheel is known as life at the center, and of wholeness peace, plenty, harmony, and joy.

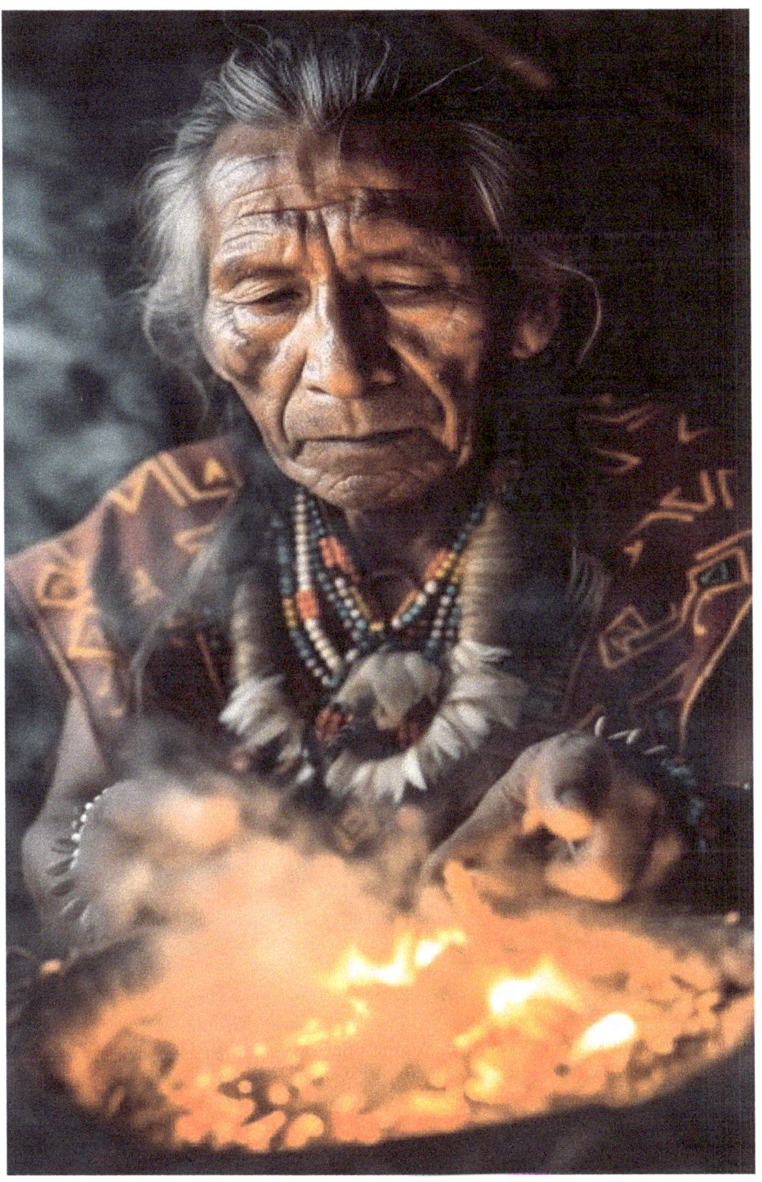

It is said that when you discover most of your current characteristics are in one direction, this is your beginning place. If that position on the medicine wheel is, for example East, following the power number four, the next direction to explore would be the West, then the North, and then the South. Once you have mastered each direction you can go home to the Center to life with the Creator....you may leave the center, at any time you wish to revisit any one of the other directions to strengthen a characteristic, and then return to the Center to live.

Application

"Two paths are available to us. One is a dark and anxious way. Those who follow it see the Earth only as a resource to be exploited. Their guide is gold or the hope of it. On this path, their Nurturing Mother will become the Witch Mother and destroy them.

The other is the Medicine Wheel Path. It is the Way of the Peace Chiefs. All those who tread it hold the land in trust. Their every act is out of stewardship and service to Mother Earth and Father Sky and all living creatures. It is both a way of Joy and Sadness, and it is endlessly satisfying..."

Quoted by: Donato Cianci and Suzanne Nadon/Walking the Medicine Wheel Path In Daylight.

The Medicine Wheel card has come to you in this reading to encourage you to explore another path to follow. Not instead of your base belief, but, as well as. When your belief system doesn't seem to feed you completely, Natures path and the teachings there will. The Medicine Wheel is a wonderful place to begin your journey.

There are many teachers on this and other paths, such as the Seth Teachings, Ted Andrews, Susan Weed, Emannuel's Books, Starhawk, Barbara Walker, Mary Summer Rain, Christine Northrup MD, Marianne Williamson, Jan Phillips, Michael

Harner, Jamie Sans, and so many more. Enjoy the journey!

I wanna know what the Medicine Wheel has to say to me tonight,
I wanna know what the Medicine Wheel has to say to me tonight,
I have opened my heart wide to hear Great Spirit calling,
I have laughed and I have cried through every lesson's learning.
I will bless what the Medicine Wheel has to say to me tonight,

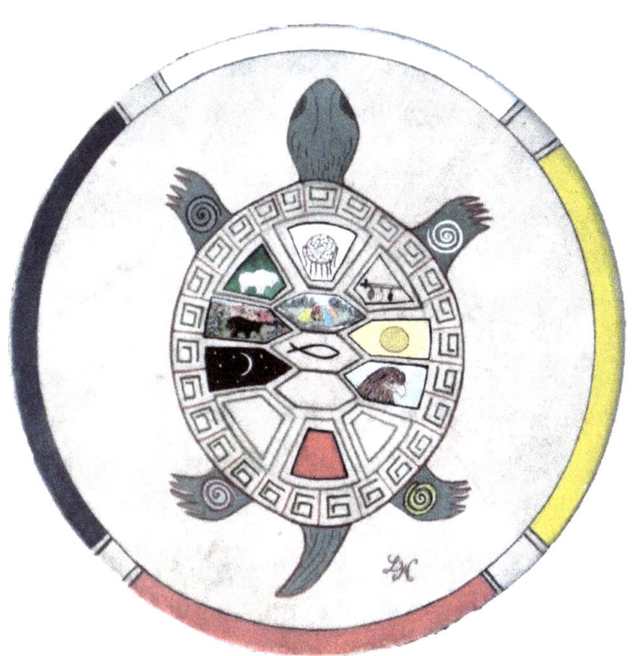

20. The Yin and Yang

We are all born of a Mother, and can be either, Yin or Yang but always both. Because we are of the fluids of a male and the fluids of a female we hold attributes of both male and female within. Sometimes as a male we spot the female side in ourselves and sometimes as a female we see our male side emerge. This is the Yin and Yang. The white spot, inside the black side, the Yin being the male in every female, and the black spot in the white Yang side symbol, being the female in every male

Yin (the black section of the symbol) represents shadows, feminine energy, and generally the more mysterious side of things. Yang (the white section of the symbol) represents the sun, masculine energy, and things that are more out in the open.

The symbol is balanced perfectly, and the curved line reminds us that in oneness there is no division. When unrest of any kind disrupts oneness, balance needs to be restored. Energies need to be aligned in order for there to be harmony once again for everything in the Universe that lives. Our flow is the flow of our Universe. Everything affects everything.

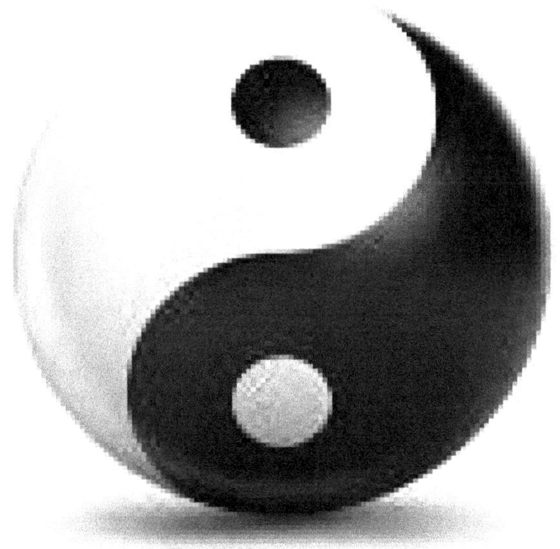

Application

Yin and Yang comes to you in a reading to remind you that the imbalance that sits within you at this time has disrupted your world, your universe long enough. It is time to take this matter into hand and find balance. No one else but you can correct this unrest.

Merging the Mind – Yang – Male, with the Heart – Yin -Female, will help you tremendously. One way to do this is to speak and listen for one whole day only from your mind, your computer data place. And then spend the entire next day speaking and listening only with your Heart. The various ways you will understand everything you speak and hear will amaze you. Balance should be restored, and then one won't be working against the other. Disparity will manifest as physical illness, depression or anxiety when one goes through life unbalanced. And many do.

These are the energies to work on...to balance.

Yang/ Strong/Male Energy– Logic/analysis, confidence, dominant, action, protect, discipline, firmness, speaking, thinking, air/fire elements, warmth.

Yin/Female/Sensitive Energy – Emotional, apprehensive, passive, feeling, nurture, understand, compassion, softness, listening, earth/water elements, coolness.

Yoga and or Meditation are wonderful ways to balance Yin and Yang energies daily.

Gift yourself with balance and speak and hear everything in a brand new light.

Namaste'

21. The Original Mother

A meditation I enjoy doing for a Circle of Women is 'The Original Mother'. We establish our breathing first, focusing on taking in a long deep breath, in through our nose and a long exhale out through our mouth...extending the full breaths in, and extending the breaths out. We do this for about five minutes. If you aren't practising this method each day for five minutes, then you should be doing it three times a day for an hour.

Now that you are completely relaxed we begin...I ask them to imagine a large Circle of Women outside in a sunny spot in a meadow of wildflowers. In a clockwise motion, starting with yourself, see your Mother take you up into her arms and pass you to her Mother. And then she passes you to her Mother. Then she passes you to her Mother. Continuing, she, passes you to her Mother, and she passes you to her Mother. She passes you to her Mother, and she, passes you to her Mother, and her Mother passes you to her Mother. She passes you to her Mother, and then she passes you to her Mother, who in turn passes you to her Mother, and she passes you to her Mother...and she passes you to the Original Mother.

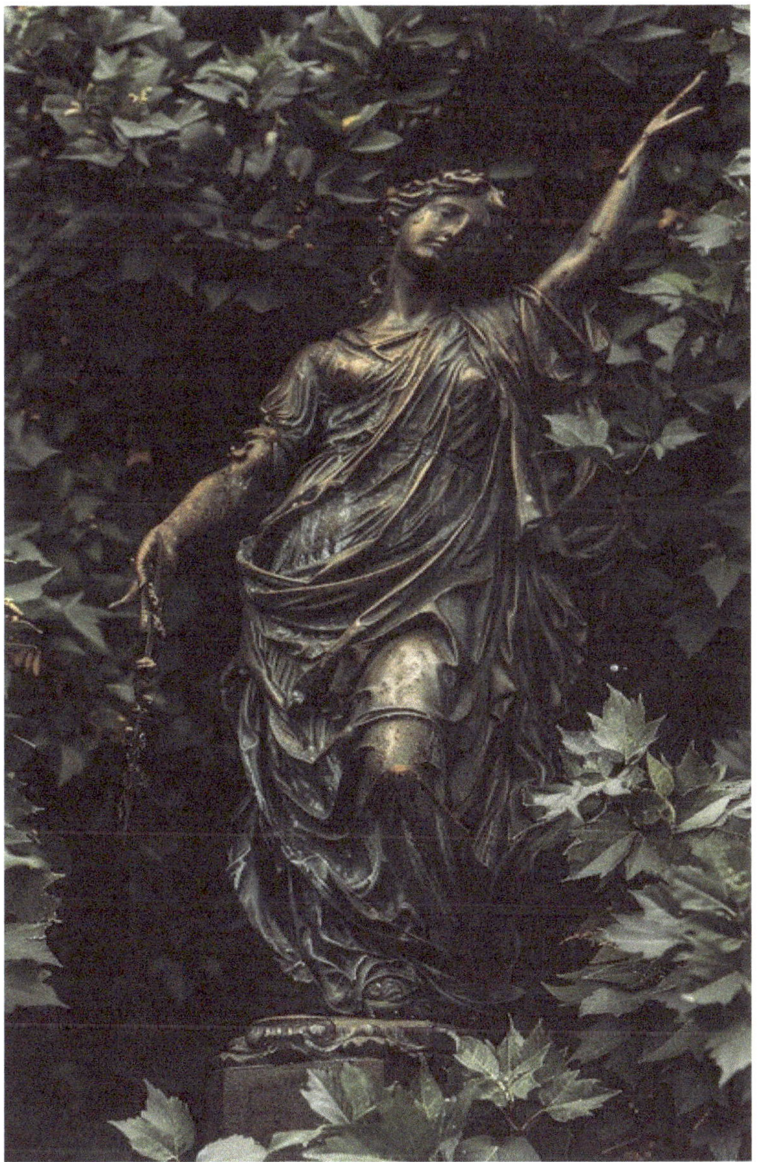

You look into one another's eyes and you ask a question that has been burning within you, without an answer for most of your life. Without speaking, her eyes give you the answer you have always wanted.

Then, The Original Mother passes you to her Daughter, and she passes you to her Daughter. She then passes you to her Daughter who passes you to her Daughter. She passes you to her Daughter and she passes you to her Daughter then passes you to her Daughter, so that she can pass you to her Daughter, and she passes you to her Daughter. Then she passes you to her Daughter and she passes you to her Daughter, and she passes you to her Daughter, and she gently passes you to her Daughter. She then passes you to her Daughter and she passes you to her Daughter.

Before all the Mothers and Daughters depart they take hands and chant....

"And may all Mothers know that they are loved, and may all Sisters know that they are strong, and may all Daughters know that they are beautiful, that the Circle of Women will go on...that the Circle of Women will go on. Wey hey ya, Wey hey ya, Wey hey hey hey ya. Wey hey ya, Wey hey ya, Wey hey hey hey ya..."

Application

If The Original Mother has stepped into your reading today, you are being put on notice that the Unconditional Love that your Mother has for you, whether she is still with you on this planet or whether she continues her journey in the Divine Realm now, is the same Unconditional Love that you have for your children. If you haven't children, then you automatically are an Auntie Or Uncle to all children...a profound role and responsibility to hold close to your heart.

The way to get this done is to set your intention and commit to ending the madness and assisting our Mother the Earth in righting herself. The Divine in me Bows to the Divine in you.

22. Grandmother Moon

People of ancient times followed the cycles of the Moon, knowing that she affected the seasons and of our own bodies. When the Moon was New her gravity affected the tides just as much as the Full Moon did. But it was when the Moon was New, just a sliver in the Western night's sky that Woman made their way to the Moon Lodge to bleed together, for three days. The gravity pulled their blood down and out of their bodies, and out onto the moss floor, and then trickled through the moss into the Earth as a way to thank the Earth for her bounty, reaffirming their oneness with the Earth and with the Moon. In those times there was no artificial light to interrupt their menstrual cycles, all was a natural flow. All was one. Women in those times weren't conditioned to believe that their bleeding was a curse. In fact, Women were conditioned to believe that their bleeding was a life giving gift.

Many cultures associate the moon with feminine aspects of life, such as birth, growth, and renewal. It's also seen as a symbol of the cyclical nature of life, with its phases representing the different stages of a woman's life, from menstruation to pregnancy to childbirth.

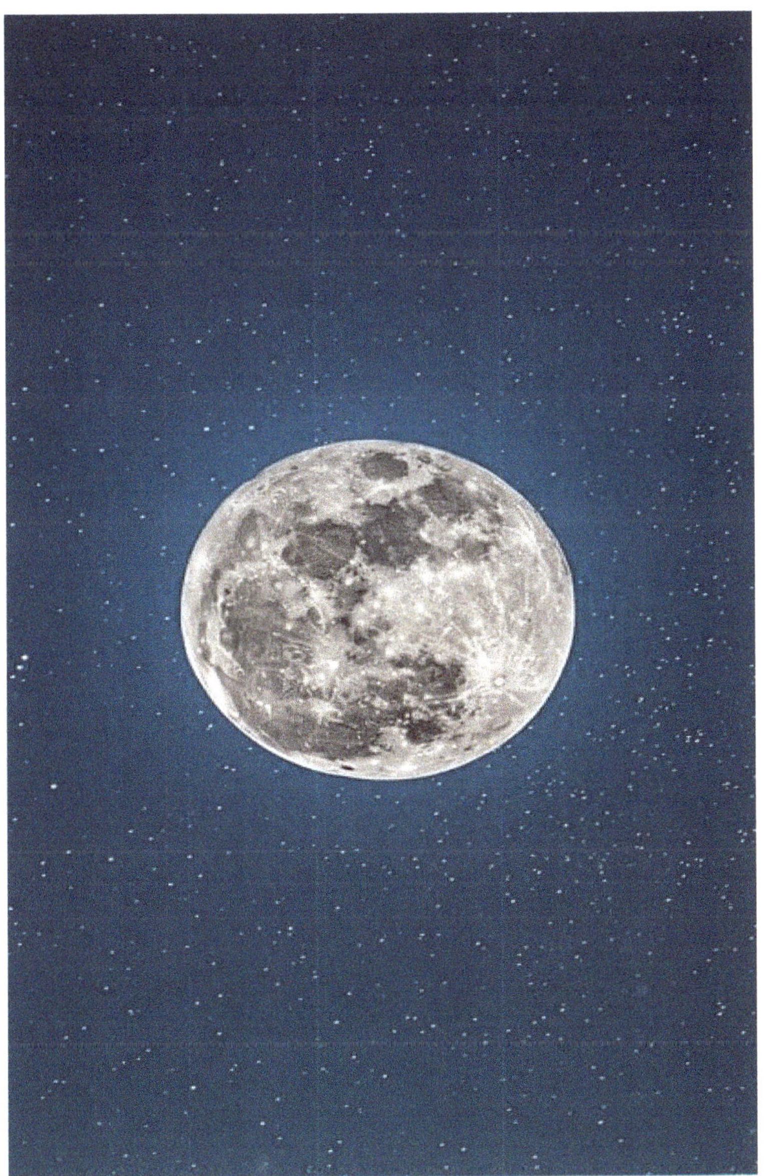

The Moon is always there, watching, steadfast, knowing us in our light and dark moments, changing forever just as we do.

Every day it's a different version of itself. Sometimes weak, sometimes strong and full of light, and she always shows us the same face. The moon understands what it means to be human.

Oh Moon Mother Light of the Night
The Stars Who are your Company Dance with you,
Teach me the Mystery of Your Dance,
That we May Be in Harmony with You.
Learn to Give Away and Renew.

Application

Grandmother Moon dances into your reading with Love. She is always here to light your path, no matter where you go. Notice the affects that she has on you and your body. Notice your body waxing and waning within her dance. When you are out of step, or that your cycle is interrupted you may want to take note of the direction your sleeping place faces. Does the Moon shine on your face while you sleep? Or do street lights or other artificial means block your view of her, and she of you? If this is true for you its best to move your sleeping place to somewhere you can bask in her glory all night long. This will coordinate your cycles with hers and correct any and all interruptions/disturbances you are suffering from.

Think of the Women in ancient times and realize the perfect synchronicity that they lived with, that was theirs. Match that wisdom with your own, and your body, mind and spirit will thank you.

The thirteenth moon of Creation is Big Spirit Moon. Its purpose is to purify us, and to heal all of Creation, a process which may take a three month long spiritual journey. During this time, we receive instructions on the healing powers of the universe and transform into our own vision of the truth. May It Be So.

23. Medicine Name

One beautiful warm and sunny afternoon, one that really should have been enjoyed in the out of doors, I chose to attend a conference at the Holiday Inn on Addictions. At the time I had a private practice as an Addiction Educational Consultant. This conference would assist me in affording me more methods and insights in my practice. Although I have walked Alcoholism myself and grew up in an alcoholic home acquiring a vast amount of knowledge there, it was good for my practice to remain informed about any new techniques counsellors may be using then. It was at this conference, during the opening ceremony in a beautiful prayer, I found my Medicine Name. As soon as I heard it I knew it was mine....Singing Stream. My Great Grandmother was Native, born on the Dokis First Nation in north western Ontario and was adopted into a family named Tinsdale near Golden Valley. My Medicine name still feels like it's been mine since I was a wee girl...but in natural fact it was swimming around in my DNA. I found it difficult to remain focused on the opening prayer after finding that beautiful name.

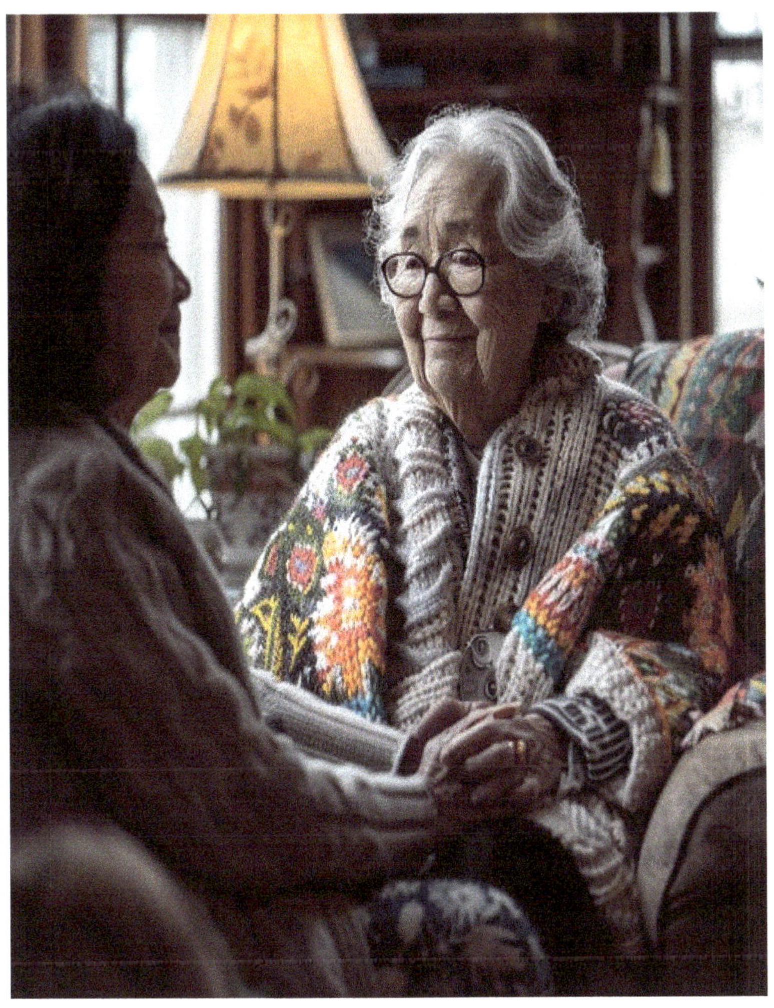

It came to pass that within the Women's Healing Circles that I hosted weekly, I began noticing that the various characteristics of the Women were showing up on the Medicine Wheel prompting me to search further to try and find their Medicine Names. It came to pass that within the Women's Healing Circles that I hosted weekly, I began noticing that the various characteristics of the Women were showing up on the Medicine Wheel prompting me to search further to try and find their Medicine Names. When the time was right, one by one I would discover the beginning places of these Women, meaning, the majority of their characteristics in one particular direction on the wheel. Following the teachings of my colleague Suzanne Nadon in her book Walking the Medicine Wheel in Daylight I discovered that once a person's beginning place is established, the power number four holds the direction to go next to master all the characteristics of the Medicine Wheel allowing you to eventually live at the center with the Creator. For example, if a person's beginning gift is in the East, looking at the shape of the power number four, her next challenge will be to master the West direction's characteristics. Then to the North, and finally to the South. The Woman's Medicine Name I was seeking, came to me once I knew her beginning gift. It was fascinating for me, and very well received by the Women. In ceremonies such as Sweat Lodges, or in Healing Circles/Drumming Circles, she would use her Medicine Name. When I gave a Woman her name we would do it in a ceremony. We sat facing one another, cross legged, and gazed into one another's eyes. I would explain how her Beginning Gift was found, and where she needed to travel next, and then I said, "Blessed be your Medicine Name ________." Much more formal than the way my name came to me.

Application

If the Medicine Name card has come to you today in your reading, it's time to honour yourself even more than you ever have been honoured before. Within sacred space, among those of like mind and heart, you too can find and share your Medicine Name. I believe we all have one, and to realize that and access this gift is most gratifying.

Your Medicine Name is a sacred connection with your Spirituality and is considered formal in a very meaningful way. All that you know to be true rings out to anyone that also carries this sacred gift. Even at first meetings, your Medicine Name speaks to the person you are meeting in such a way that they know you well upon hearing it. They honour your journey, and honour your truth, immediately and naturally.

You are being guided to learn the Medicine Wheel teachings, and discover your sacred spiritual self there. Hold your head high and when you are in the presence of those of like mind and like heart, use your Medicine Name. Blessed Be.

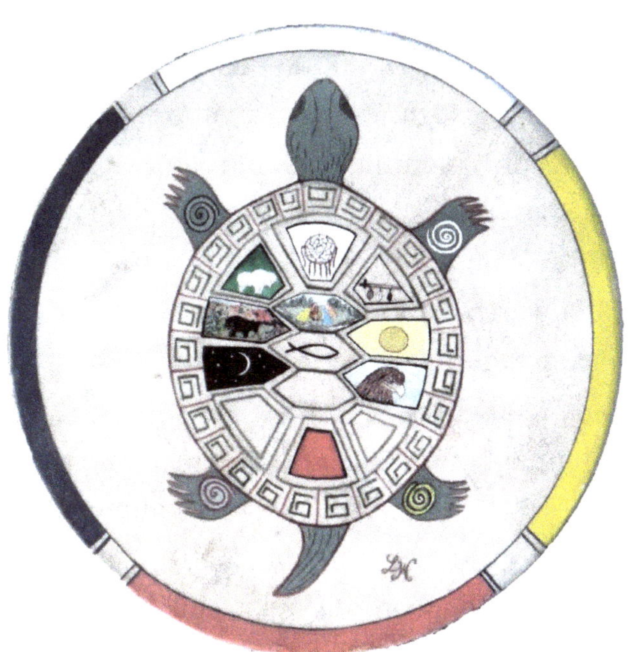

24. Warrior Shield

We all have those days when we feel incapable of dealing, unworthy of love...low self esteem. I always say that its 'at those times that we are clearly wearing our 'hurt child shield' which isn't much of a shield at all.' While helplessness washes over us, we do wear it...wear it so obviously that others recognize it, and often treat us accordingly.

It is at these times that its important to know that you needn't continue seeing yourself in such a light...but rather, as a strong, capable, confident warrior woman or man. All it takes is the desire to wear a warrior's shield and let others see strength in your character and fire in your eyes, ready to take on any challenge.

In meditation, take yourself to a time in your life when you looked and felt absolutely gorgeous, oozing confidence, strength and grace, dressed in your most beautiful dress or suit...picture her\him and while you have that picture in your mind, press your thumb and your forefinger together, and then let go. If you do this three times a day for a week you'll find that all you will have to do in the future is, press your thumb and your forefinger together and he\she will appear.

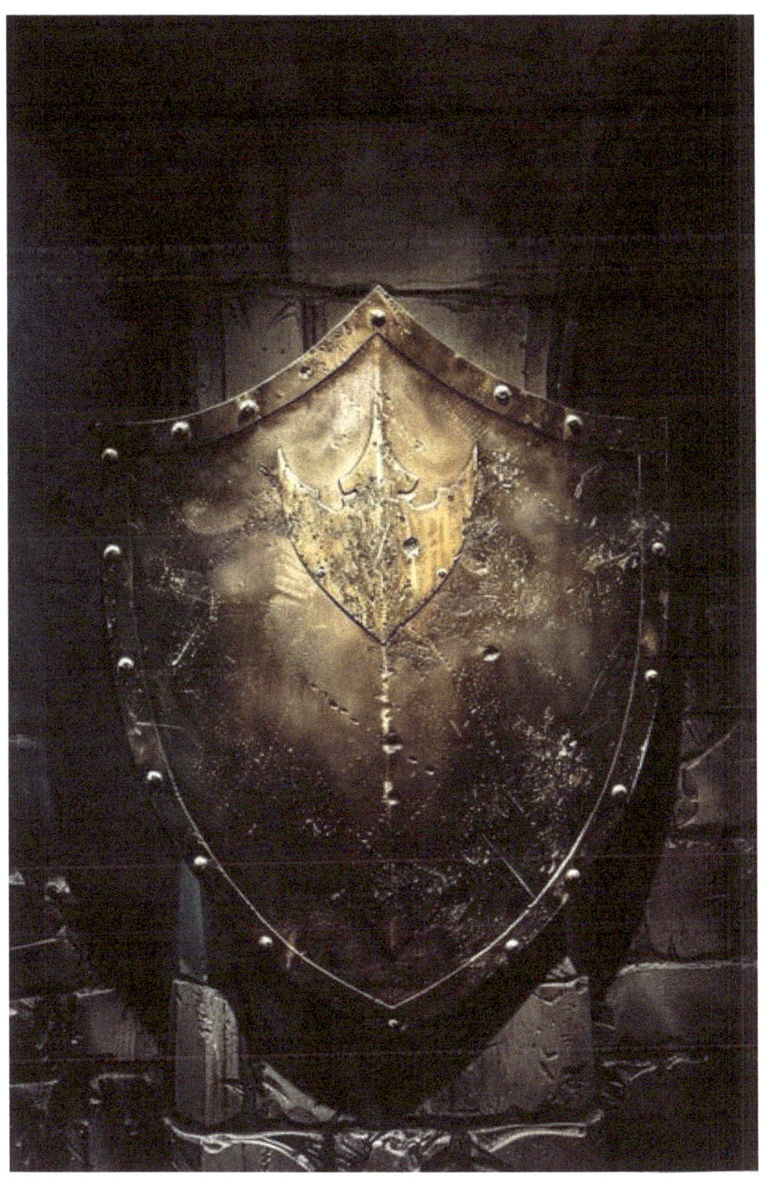

It is then, that you may push down the 'hurt child shield' and bring forward, over your head, your warrior shield. This is the shield that others will see and react accordingly.

This is the shield that speaks, saying, "don't even think about running me down or treating me badly." Raise your chin and allow your fire to show in your eyes, balanced beautifully with unmistakable grace. You will speak of unwavering strength and beauty beyond compare.

I Am My Mother's Savage Daughter
The one that runs barefoot cursing sharp stones,
I am my Mother's savage daughter,
I will not cut my hair, I will not lower my voice.

Sarah Hester Ross

Application

My thoughts immediately go to a beautiful Mohawk Woman that attended one of my Workshop Weekends. She sat with her head down, as though ashamed of her Native-ness. Particularly since she was Mohawk and this was the same year that the uprising took place in Oka, Mohawk territory. The powers that be were attempting to take sacred burial grounds away from Oka and build a golf course. The Mohawk stood up and fought the authorities off their land. A 78-day standoff (11 July – September 26 1990) between Mohawk protesters, Quebec police and the Canadian Army. The Mohawk won. One police officer was killed in the crisis.

As I observed this Mohawk Woman, I could see that her shame for what she believed others thought of her, and who she was, steadily grew. It was then that I spoke up and asked her to put the backs of her fingers on her right hand under her chin, and raise her chin. Then I told her that my name for her will be Mohawk Woman and then I said, "When you say the words Mohawk Woman, when you come to 'Woman," slide your fingers forward and into the air, and keep your chin up. Then, all the participants did it with her. All of them proceeded to push down the shield they wore when they arrived for the retreat, and bring forward, over their heads, their

Warrior Shields. When you draw this card in a reading it speaks to a place within you that feels unaccepted, certainly by yourself and by others. Push down that shield, and bring forward your Warrior Shield, now.

May it be So.

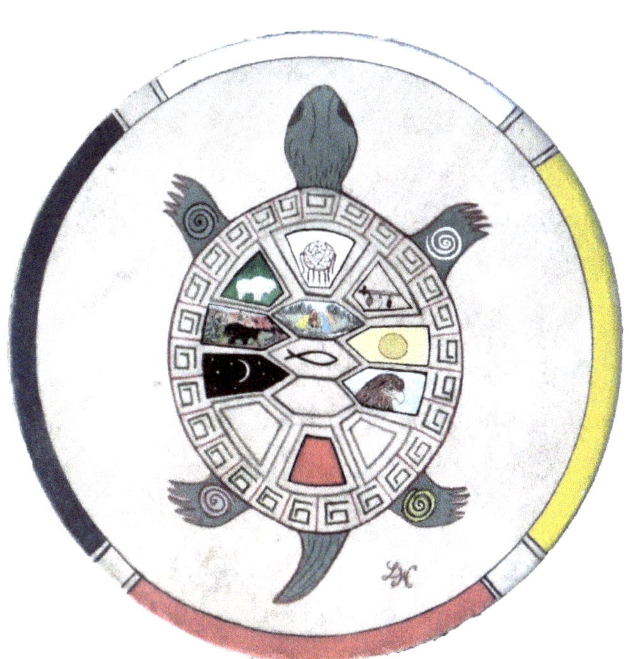

25. Dousing with a Pendulum

Dousing is a method of Divination used to gain insight into a question or situation.

To begin you will want to establish with your pendulum what will be a yes answer or a no answer to your question. This is done by holding the ring at the end of your pendulum so that the pendulum can freely move in the direction that you have established will be yes or no. To do this, hold the pendulum in your left hand (your information coming in side) and dangle it, holding it between your index finger and your thumb. It's common to hold your opened right hand a few inches below the end of your pendulum if you please. Ask the pendulum how it will move to give you the answer 'yes.' Once the pendulum connects with your energy it will either swing north to south or east to west or sometimes it will move in a circular motion. Then once that is established ask the pendulum what movement it will make for you if the answer to your question is 'no.' You can also ask it what movement it will make for 'maybe' if you like. It's always wise not to ask it questions that you already know the answer to. I find that my pendulum doesn't move at all if I do this.

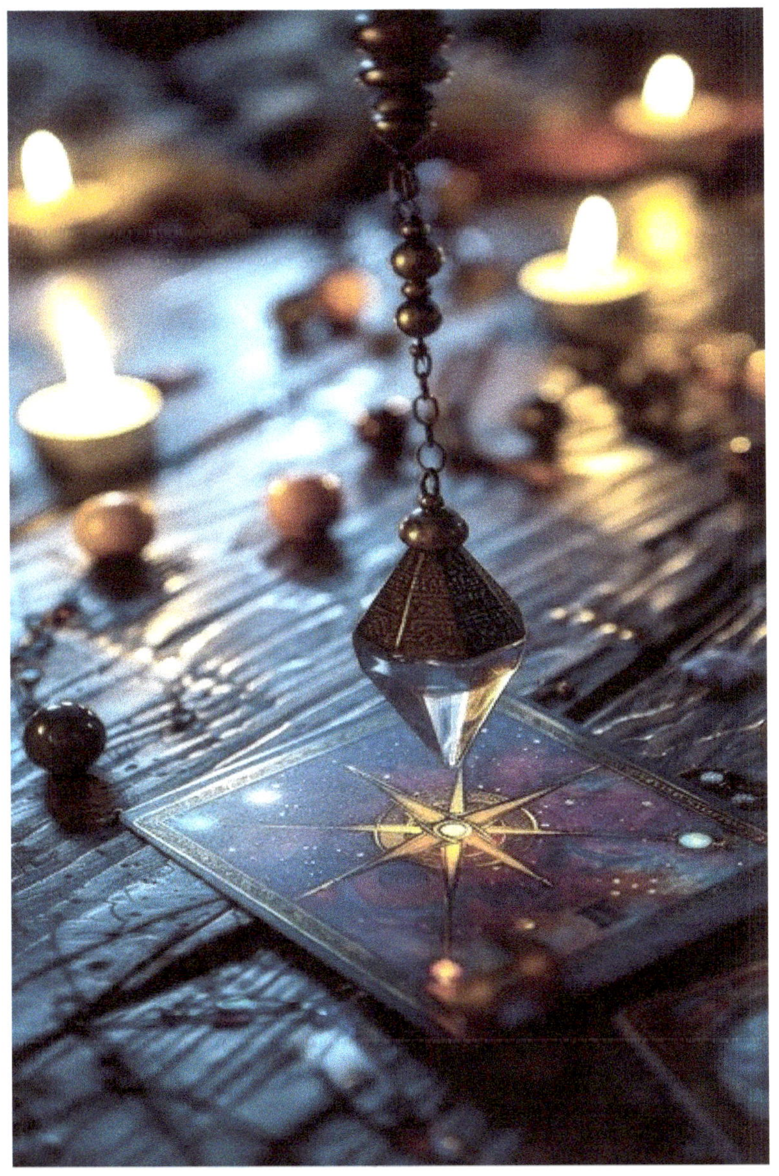

You could ask if it didn't move because you already know that answer. Once your directions are established you can begin.

Always, when beginning your time with your pendulum, it's most appropriate to say:

"I call upon my higher self to answer these questions. I seek only truthful answers, which are aligned with the highest and greatest good for all concerned."

When asking about health outcomes or diagnosis it's not recommend that you take the information as gospel...rather, one should seek these answers as well, from your health professional.

Often folks will set the stage as you might for a Tarot Card reading. You may wish to light a candle, burn some sage, set down a favourite cloth to dowse over, and or play your favourite meditation music. You might even want to set your favourite treat along side you. Whatever it is that creates your time with your pendulum a sacred time, do that.

As when you do a reading for yourself or another, it's best to turn off all devices and have a private place to do your work, as to prevent any interruptions. Blessed Be!

Application

It's not uncommon to be undecided about things you would like to know a simple 'yes' or 'no' or even 'maybe' answer to. Should you choose to give your pendulum the opportunity to answer you by having a movement for 'rephrase' this is perfectly fine. If you don't have a pendulum to dowse with a piece of thread and a cork is suitable.

It's advisable that you give yourself all of the options that are available to you that connects with, and speaks to, your energy alone.

Drawing this card generally signals that you have options that you may not know of and that your energy is actually more accurate than many other ways of affirming what you have been pondering. This card is saying to you, "be assured that this method of divination is a powerful tool for you to access," and that "your energy is a critical tool, that can definitely provide you with valid answers." Dive in with confidence! May It Be So!

There is a secret One Inside,
All the stars and all the Galaxies
Run through your hands like beads.

26. Leading With Your Heart

My Minister and myself and a prior acquaintance wanted to start a Mental Health outreach group in our community. Some time later another acquaintance agreed to be one of the four leaders and turned out to be our primary financial supporter. In fact, her Son had taken his life and had previously started a Mental Health awareness group in town called, "Lead With Your Heart.". We adopted the name for our group and interestingly our first meeting drew thirty-three people from our community. I attended every meeting for over three plus years. My Minister would get called away fairly often with congregational needs. One of the other leaders came as much as possible, and our primary supporter attended few meetings.

We discovered that a very good established counselling group in town called Archway offered our people counselling sessions on sliding scale fee of $30 per hour and Lead With Your Heart could handle that easily. Some of our people required more than six sessions so the church also gave six sessions to them. Others needed even more, and this was discussed between the four leaders and agreed to.

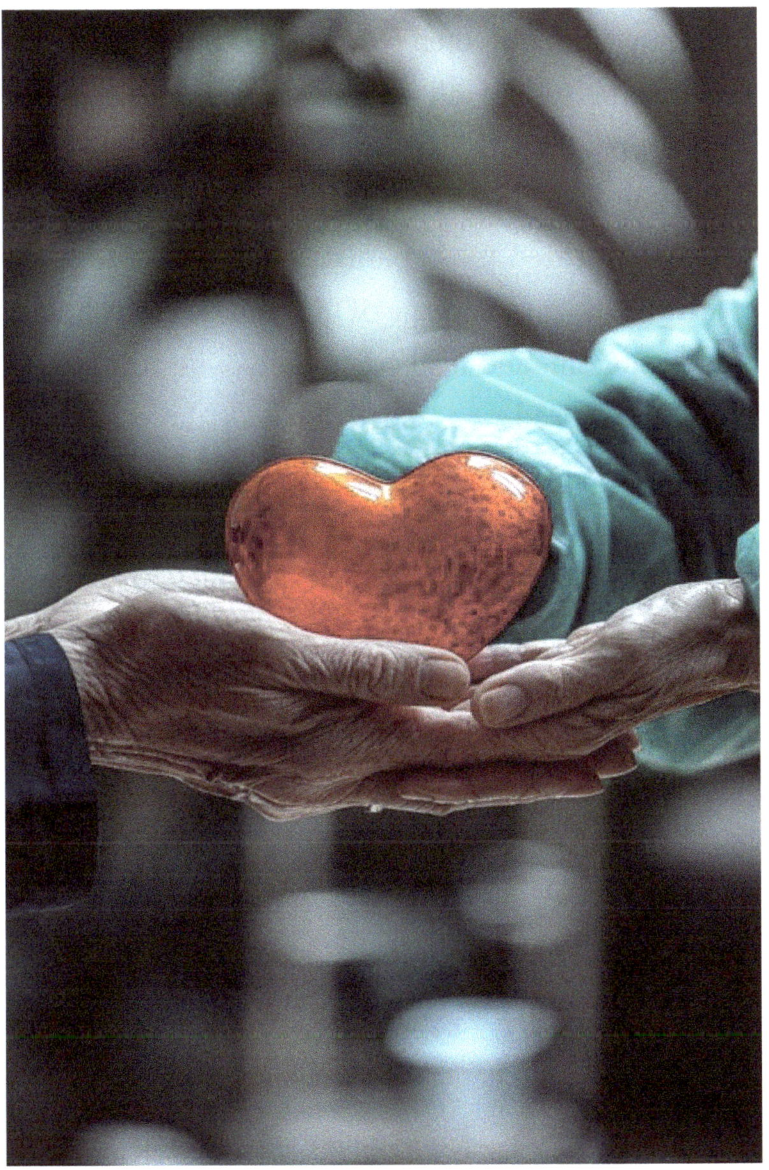

I remember pushing for more for a couple of our attendees and was met will a wee bit of opposition but they were outvoted by the other three leaders.

I actually did all the administration and the promotional work for our group as well. My Minister and myself were actually the two that easily identified those participants that came to us with great needs, and one of them coined the phrase, we 'leaned in' and lead completely with our hearts. As time passed, we ended up with three leaders, instead of four. We offered Art classes lead by one of our friends that actually came in one evening and lead a program sharing her art, and her story about how art helped her heal after a traumatic time. The art classes were run weekly each month and were always booked solid. Lead With Your Heart supplied all the paints, brushes, and canvases and the church provided the space. For those who couldn't afford the cost that we paid the Art leader, Lead With Your Heart sponsored them as well. We ran our programs once per month for three+ years until Covid came along and we had to stop all our groups.

A labour of love not only feeds those that depend on your help, but it also feeds you, generously. As my Minister always says, 'we are here to be the hands and feet of Jesus'. We are here to help one another, and ultimately 'Lean In'...So Mote It Be.

Application

How many times have you 'Leaned In' to really hear and feel another's pain, be it physical or emotional, or even a spiritual emptiness? How many times have you needed just that yourself?

When things happen in your life that literally break you, have you ever heard yourself say 'where was the Creator in that? How do I continue to believe in a merciful being above, when things like this happen?' The answer is simple...look to the helpers. Look around at the ones that are there to assist with all they have to give. Lean In! Has your heart and soul been warmed by another that really listened to you? That leaned in to find the places that needed the most assistance within you? Be the change you want to see in this world? The rewards are many and the friendships created are lasting, unwavering and steadfast. Open your heart as you would wish to be assisted. Always be the hands and feet. Lean In.

The Tender Lady has sadness in her eyes,
She's seen the fallen hopes, the loneliness and lies
Tell me have you something to ease her pain?
Why not give her happiness, and peace again?

I'm just a friend of hers, I cannot move the stars.
But the Tender Lady reads messages like ours,
Tell me you have you something to ease her pain?
Why not give her happiness, and peace again?

I know I've come before asking things for me, but
the
Tender Lady needs so much care you see.
Tell me have you something to ease her pain?
Why not give her happiness, and peace again?

Music, oh sweet melody, won't you hold her close
to you,
And comfort her, for me?

27. Soul Retrieval

A Shamanic technique, Soul Retrieval is done for people that have had great trauma in their lives, that stays with them, generally for life. This level of trauma, often referred to as Post Traumatic Stress Disorder is absolutely crippling. Without intervention PTSD can lead to devastating outcomes, including suicide. When a trauma of this magnitude happens it's believed, within Shamanic teachings, that parts of a person's Soul leaves the body, and remains in the place where the trauma occurred. A trained professional can undertake a Shamanic Journey to the place where this Soul part resides ever since the trauma occurred, and bring it back to the patient, returning wholeness to their lives once again. All that is required by the patient is to remain present without falling asleep. The practitioner will lie down beside them touching only at the shoulder, the hip and the ankle. A drummer will drum for this Journey, the same way they drum for a regular Shamanic Journey, with a moderately slow beat, keeping the Shaman connected to ordinary reality by the sound of the drum beat.

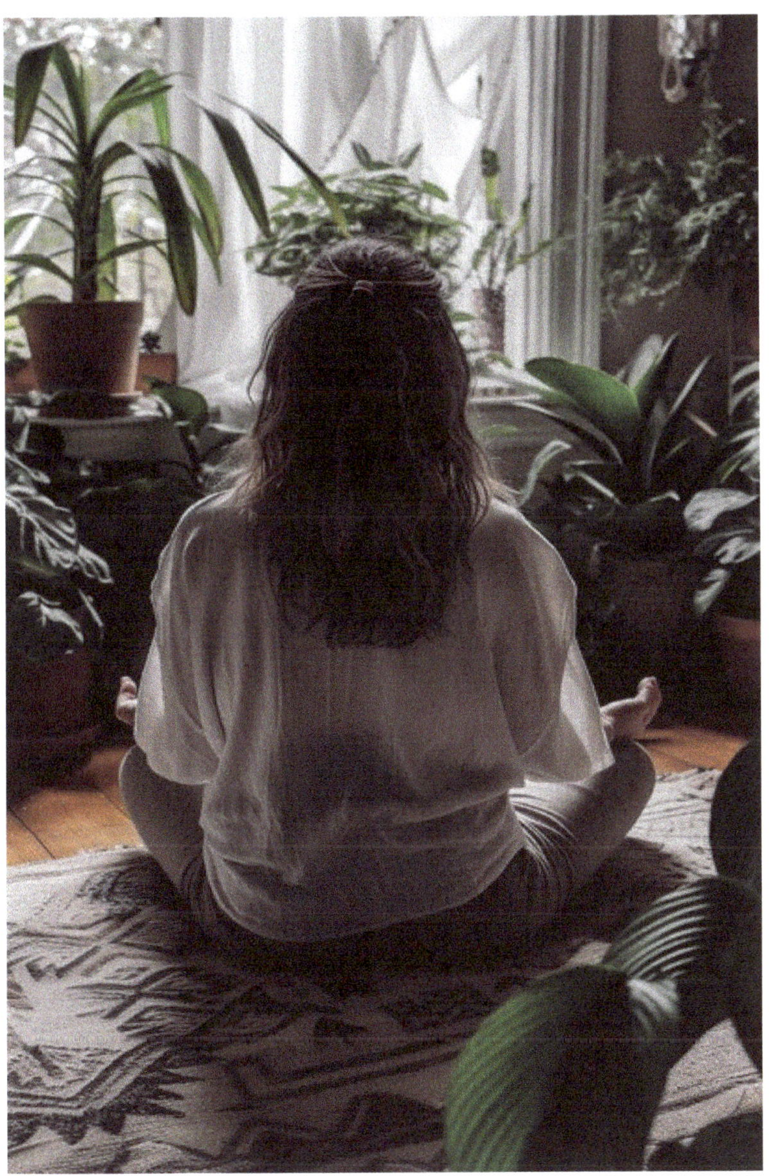

The Shaman will hold a crystal in their hand and this will be used as the vehicle in which the Soul part will occupy during the Journey back to its original home.

When departing for the Journey to find the missing Soul part the practitioner will meet up with their Power Animal in the lower world and travel together from there to where the Soul part is. Often the practitioner will walk into the place where the trauma took place and see everything that happened. At that time the Soul part will be invited to come with them back to the home of its Soul. It will be explained that it will greatly help the person that waits for its return. Most often the Soul part gladly agrees to accompany the practitioner and their Power animal, back home. They are carried in the crystal and the Journey home begins. There are times when the Soul part is afraid to leave, and sometimes the practitioner will have to trick it to join them. Once the Journey is over the practitioner will raise their arms out, with the crystal in hand, and back down again, three times to advise the drummer that the Journey is complete. The drummer will strike the drum seven times, four times in a row, ending the process. Then the practitioner will assist the patient in sitting up, and she will kneel behind her and place the crystal at the patient's crown chakra and blow the Soul part into that chakra three times. Then she will sit beside the patient and look into her eyes saying, 'Welcome home'. She will begin to recant the Journey careful to include every single detail to the patient. Following this she will sing:

Return again, return again, return to the home
of your Soul.
Return to where you are, return to who you are,
return to what you are,
Born and born again.

The patient will then be instructed to take loving care of this Soul part that has returned. When the Soul part is that of a child's Soul, she will be instructed to play with this part, to give her ice cream, take her to the park, do all the things with her that she missed while away. To love her, and care for her, and welcome her back with Joy. Promise to nurture her and keep her safe, forever more. This is the process of a Soul Retrieval.

The practitioner must be prepared on such a Journey to see and experience some horrific happenings. To concentrate only on retrieving the Soul part and leaving the scene as soon as possible. Sometimes the Journey takes them to places such as an abandoned well....sometimes it's a violent rape or other such violence. Whatever the case, the focus must remain with the Soul part's Journey home. Wholeness is once more restored, with love, compassion and caring. So Mote It Be.

Application

When drawing the Soul Retrieval card, you are being put on notice that when such a trauma happened to you or someone you love, in their lifetime, until this method is executed the space within, where the Soul part lived in their Soul, there will remain a void. That void will be cleared of this unrest prior to the Soul Retrieval by the practitioner. This is called 'Shamanic surgery.' Symbolically this space will be cleared of any debris or dis-ease that has taken up residence there, for the Soul part to returned to. If you feel you may have a condition that could be resolved, it would be recommended that you undergo such a procedure. It is not as difficult as you might think to locate a Soul Retrieval practitioner.

All that is required is that you believe that this process will be of benefit to you. Seek, and you shall find. Wholeness is always a refreshing gift to oneself. Be kind to yourself, and most importantly, trust.

May It Be So.

28. Love, Compassion and Caring

During our New Moon Women's Healing Circle one evening, when it was time to share with the Talking Stick in hand, I took the Talking Stick. I explained to the Circle that there is a difficult memory for me, based on a severe beating given me by my Father. This wasn't the first time, but it was definitely the worst. Knowing that he did in fact beat me, my Mother went on vacation with her friends just the same, as always. On the occasion in question, I was fifteen years old, and my Father beat me so badly I was taken to hospital. He had approached me in the kitchen as I was peeling potatoes for supper. He looked into the sink to see how I was peeling the potatoes and commented that I was peeling half of the potatoes off with the peel, wasting them. I shouldn't have, but I rolled my eyes at him. So the beating commenced. He smashed my head against the wall so many times, that eventually, I sunk down to the floor. He was afraid he had killed me or did some permanent damage. So he loaded me in the car and took me to hospital. I don't remember much, until I woke up in the hospital bed.

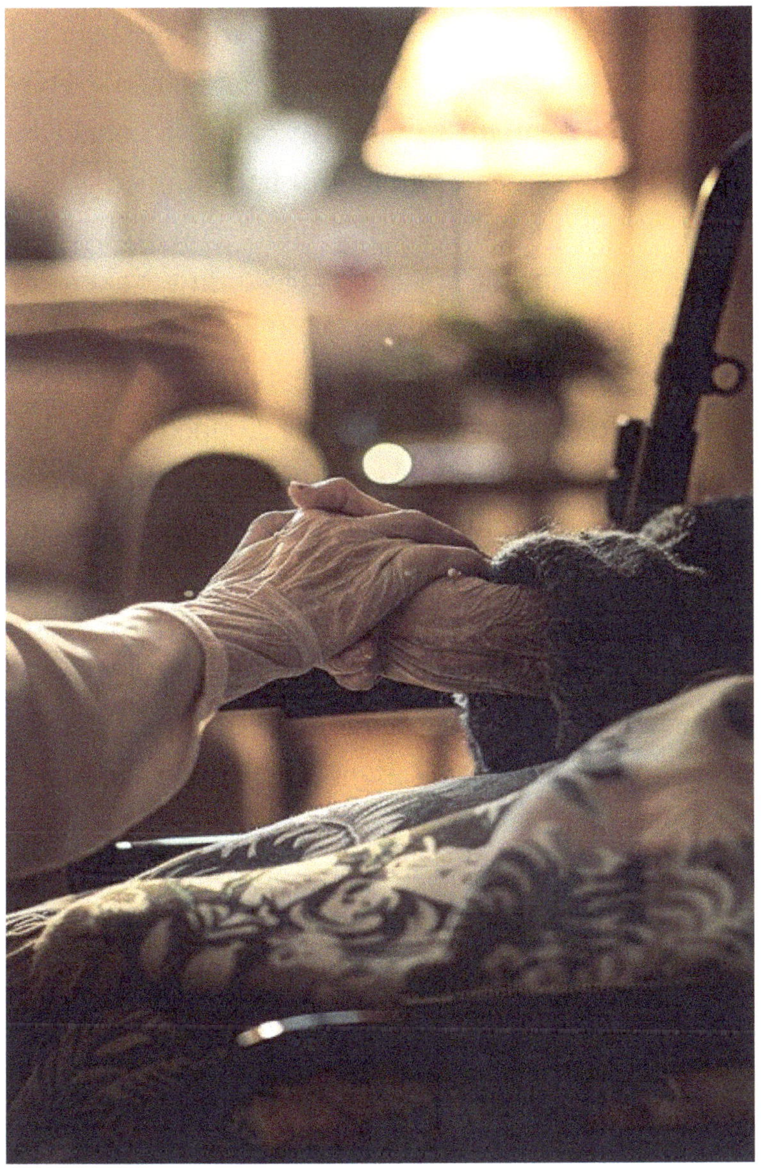

They asked me how this happened, as I put my hands through my hair on the sides of my head, and a sizable amount of hair came out with my hands. I elected to tell them how it happened. They confronted him in the hallway, and of course he denied doing it, and told them I had 'flipped'.

He was told to take me home and waken me every hour during the night. He didn't waken me even once. I didn't tell my Mother of the incident because her comment was always the same, "what did you do to deserve that?" So I stopped telling her at all. It wasn't long before I packed my things and left, to go and live with my boyfriend and his parents.

This memory repeated in my mind each and every time I peeled potatoes, until thirty years later when I had a Soul Retrieval done. Before I put the talking stick down that night, I asked the Women if they would make me a card. A card that I could go and read if that memory came into my mind ever again...any time I peeled potatoes. Each one of the Women did in fact make me a card, and I still have them all. I use them just like always, since they presented them to me at the very next New Moon Circle. All the cards express Love, Compassion, and Caring, and they comfort me, erasing the memory, and remembering my Soul Retrieval, so that I can proceed with my chore of peeling our potatoes for supper. Their Love and Compassion and Caring fill me with all three, and I am warmed and comforted every time.

This sharing wasn't the same as the other sharings in our Circle, but left permanent scars just the same as the other member's sharings did for them. We consider a Woman's sharing as her teaching, so they all thanked me for my teaching.

I was moved to train with Sandra Ingerman, a student of Michael Harner's at the Foundation for Shamanic Studies to learn Soul Retrieval. This is a technique that is explained in another card in this very deck, and is believed to return the fragmented Soul part lost, during traumatic times in our lives. To fill the space in our fragmented souls that lay void, and that can possibly be replaced by Dis-ease. Places that the fragmented soul part can return to, making us feel whole, once again. I have done Soul Retrieval for many since that training....with Love, Compassion, and Caring. Blessed Be!

Application

The Love, Compassion, Caring card encourages you to generously give the same, to any and all those that need this in their lives. For you to seek these things for yourself, wherever and whenever necessary. My prayer is that you know where that can be, or find out where you can go for this help. Naturally I recommend Soul Retrieval through reading Micheal Harner's book 'The Way of the Shaman' or Sandra Ingerman's book 'Soul Retrieval'. Learning how this is done will lead you to learning Shamanic Journeying as well, that you can easily teach someone you love and trust to perform this technique for you. How does the Universe know this? How did this card come to you? Each time you tell your story, (share your teaching), from wherever you store this story, you will feel the trauma come back up again, and your body will take on the same exact feelings, reactions (trembling, weeping, etc) as it did when the trauma happened. Wherever you store that can't help but develop into Dis-ease. That's how the Universe brought you this teaching.

Through Love, Compassion, and Caring.

May It Be So.

I will be Gentle with myself, I will Love myself,
I am a child of the Universe, being born each moment.
I will be Gentle with myself, I will Heal myself,
I am a child of the Universe, held in Love this moment.

29. Your Song

Our Healing Circle gathered one night and after we smudged, I surprised them with the theme for the evening. Every one of the women knew and loved the songs we sang at every Circle, and they knew the words well to all of them. This night we were about to make a CD of thirteen of our songs. One song after the other, no stops in between...just a Singing Stream. They didn't know which songs were picked...I simply started each one and the Women joined in. There was even laughter in our recording that night...I started a song way too high, and the words were: 'Moon Sister Moon, shining so high'...and then I sang, 'too high,' and we all laughed, and then we started the song over. It was a magical evening, and at the very next Circle one of the Women brought a bundle of CD's with her that her hubby had put together with each song having its own track. Everyone got a CD and they were in heaven. And yes, the gal's hubby left our laughter in the track! It was great!

This evening turned out to be one of our most memorable Circles. Quite often several of the Women had their own song, that they shared with us, and we added them to our repertoire.

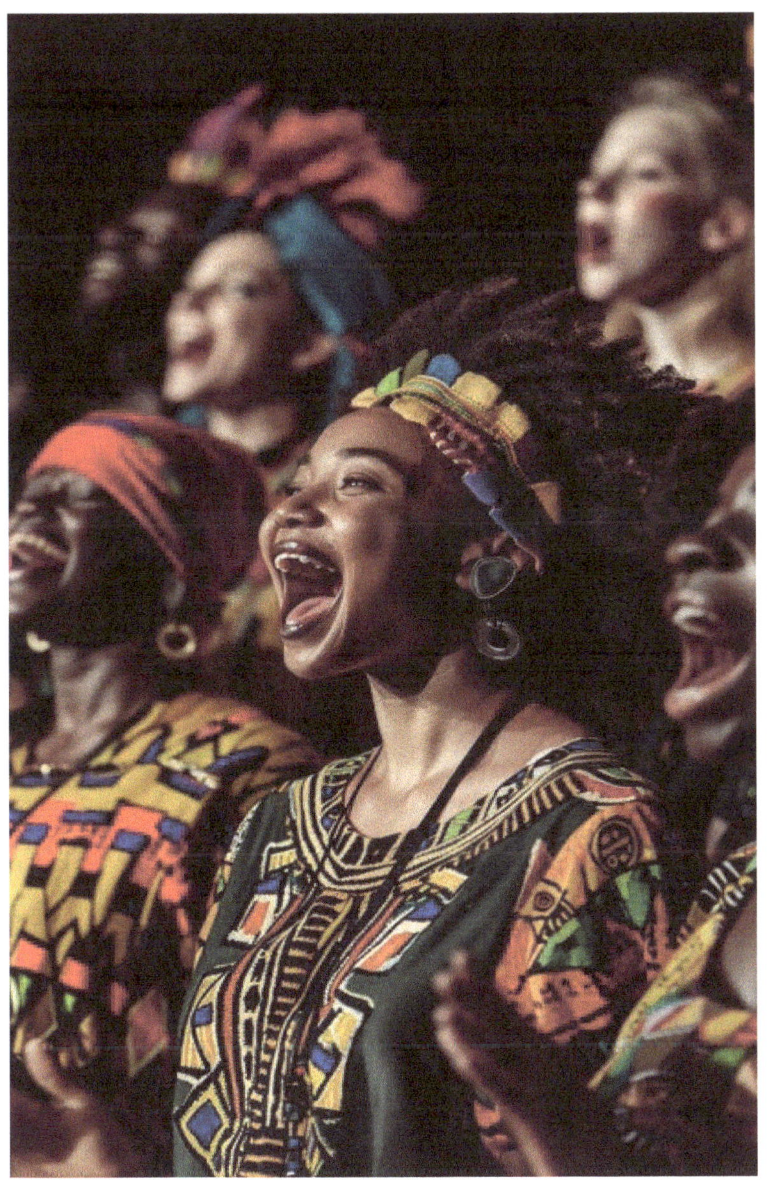

Do you have your very own song? Do you sing your song, or songs at every opportunity? Do you share your songs?

Our songs are a sacred part of our beings. It usually speaks to who we are and how we interpret our existence, our love. What is your song? So Mote It Be.

The Breath of The Goddess
Resides in my Soul
From the womb of Gaia
The Life givers unfold,
We are the Maidens, the Mothers the Crones,
And we are all Sisters
One heart and one Soul.

The Blood of The Goddess
Runs through my Bones
From the heart of Gaia
Her Warriors unfold,
We are the Fathers, the Lovers, the Sons
And we are all Brothers
Our hearts and souls One.

By-Singing Stream

Application

Sing your Song! Sing it Loud, Sing it Strong! Share your goodness with your besties, your Healing Circle or Drumming Circle, or choose to keep it for yourself. It truly is a gift to all that listen to your heart's blessings in song.

If you haven't taken a pen in hand and written your Song, choosing the Your Song card urges you to do so. Include everything you feel, write your song from your heart and revel in the beauty of your lovely self.

You can easily borrow melodies if you are new at this. Fit in your words, your feelings and your love of the things you are singing about. Most of all your song is a part of you. Beautiful you! May It Be So!

Terri's Song

Peace and Comfort in my Heart
Carry me as I depart
Serenity and truthfulness
With these things I am blessed.

30. The Record Keepers – The Stone People

Not terribly long ago, a friend joined our regular Healing Circle and she gifted me with a heart shaped stone. She remarked that a close friend of hers was having health problems and wanted her to have the heart shaped stone to remember her always. Jane paid it forward to our Healing Circle. That night we passed the stone around the Circle while each Woman meditated on it, in their hands, sending prayers for Jane's friend, asking for Spirit to bless her with whatever will be to her highest good. It was a meaningful opening to our Circle that night. We would often bring the stone out and just hold it in our hands, filling it with our energy and intent.

The Stone People are known in Native tradition as the Record Keepers. They have been here on our planet since she was created...they have seen all. Many stone people are washed up on shore from the tide's rhythm. Different people find rocks that hold the energies they need. Some people are drawn to water, some to trees, others to stones. When feeling out of balance a specific stone that a person needs will show itself.

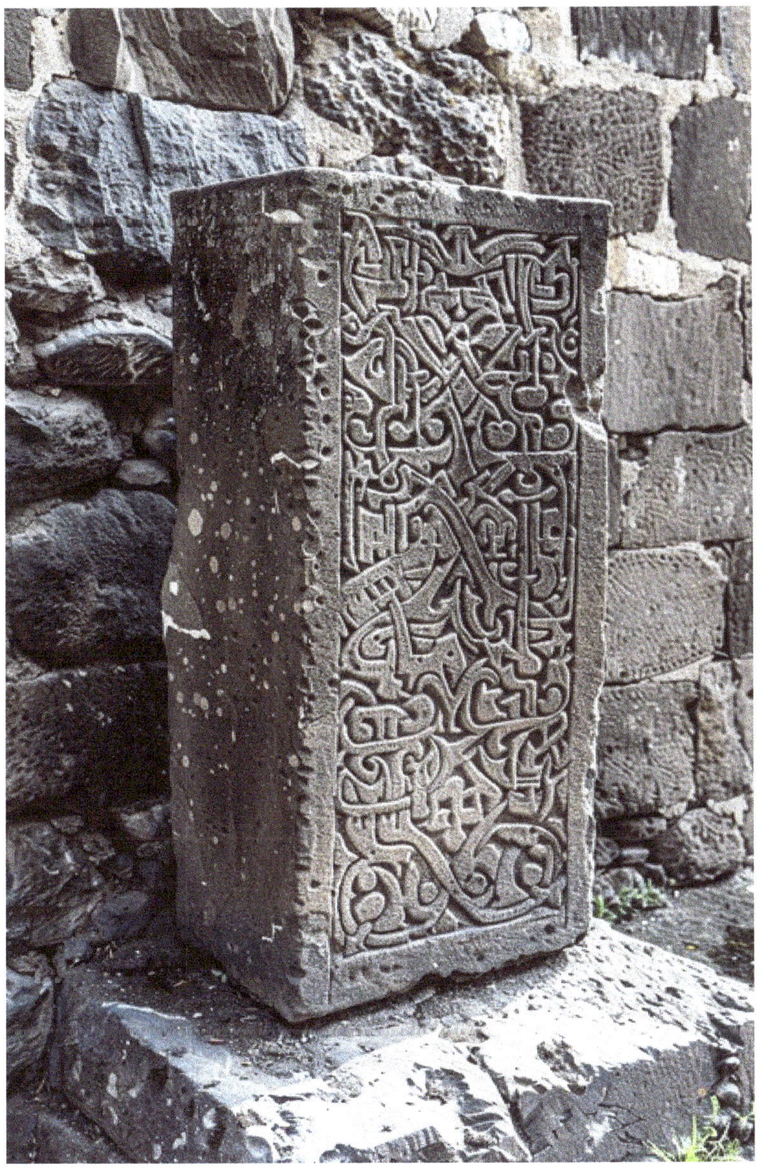

There are many healing uses in different stones... ie – Quartz brings focus and clarity, while Amethyst stones will present a third eye/protection, etc.

I use a Quartz crystal when doing a Soul Retrieval, to transport a fragmented soul part back to the person I am working with. Stones are symbolic of the history they have lived while on this Earth. They're like little history books holding memories. In many cultures rocks are symbols of luck, energy and long life too. During medieval times, people believed that you could put an emerald under your tongue and the gemstone would give you the ability to see the future.

The Stones they are Calling me,
Echoing through an eternity
Calling out to set us free
The power of the Stones.....

Application

When you draw the Record Keepers in a reading, chances are that you are feeling unbalanced, without harmony in your life, knowledge and balance. Find a stone that has appeared just for you, trusting that your stone brings the lessons you seek. Find a sacred spot outdoors and lean your back against a tree. (a Standing Person) Slow your mind and hold your stone person and breathe until you feel the unrest leave your body. This anchors you back to Mother Earth.

Your personal records are held by these libraries of rock. Memories of past lives or deja vu could bring new knowledge. Whatever the case, you are now in a position to know where you came from and where you are going.

Allow these teachers to become your Allies and discover a new world. These ancient friends are the oldest Children of Earth and only ask us to stop, and to listen.

At dawn I walked in a circle of stones
A solar temple to me yet unknown
Till by the strength of first morning light
Shown the power of the Stonehenge stones.

They grounded the energy of this place
And held us together in loving embrace
While beings of light danced above the space
Bestowing on us their wisdom and grace.

The Stones – Julie Renee

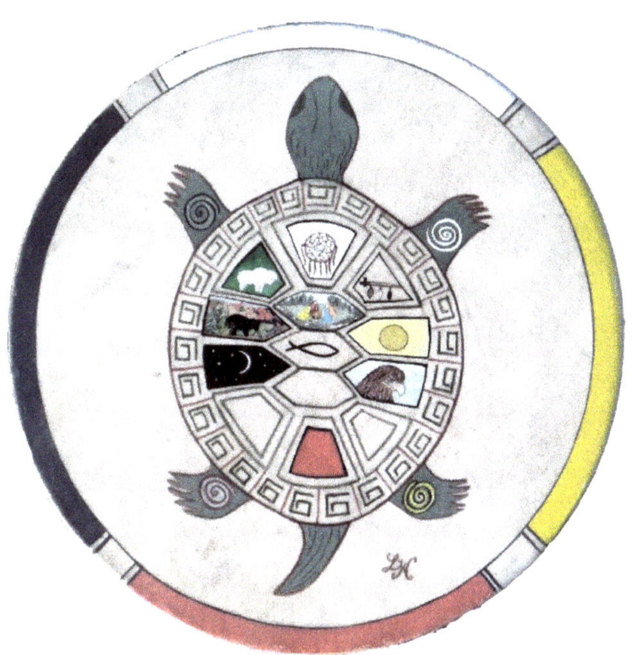

31. The Divine Feminine – Holy Spirit

The Holy Spirit – Holy Ghost...what is it? Intuition? Ah huh moments? Presence of someone or an animal spirit? Moments of grace and peace that wash over you sometimes? All of that and more?

We have heard plenty about the Father, and the Son, but the Holy Spirit/Holy Ghost doesn't get that much attention. The more I study about this segment of the holy trinity, the more my studies uncover that the Holy Spirit might just be the Divine Feminine. Before the onset of Christianity and the male God was imposed, the correct word for the highest deity was Goddess, and many temples to her glory were torn down. During the Middle Ages most of the names and titles of the Goddess were ever more minutely classified, and some were even masculinized, humanized, or diabolised. Yet such classification tend to disintegrate under deeper study that reveals the same archetypal characteristics in nearly all the "goddesses". Some people believe that a new feminine theology will emerge from the core concept lives on.

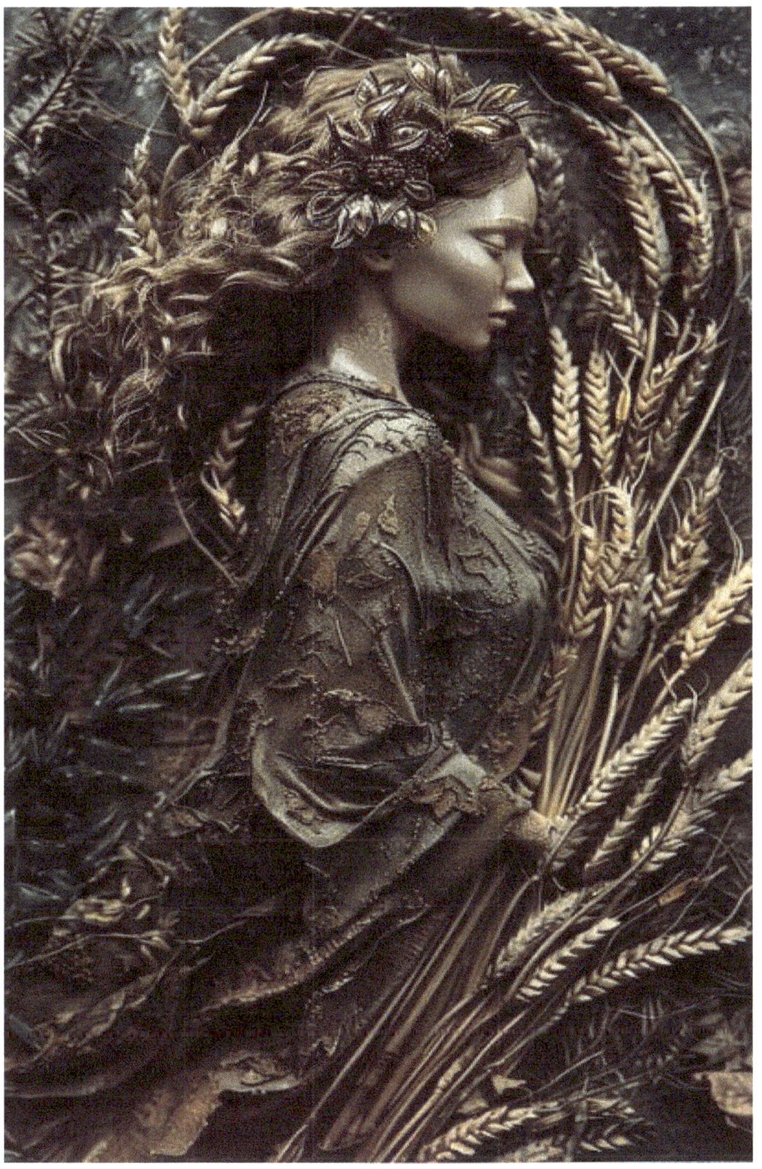

In Greek mythology Mother Nature is a common personification of nature that focuses on the life giving and nurturing aspects of nature, by embodying it, in the form of Mother. An 18th century theologian wrote "at the command of Mary all obey, even God."

Today it is widely recognized even by layman that "two rivers of common source, Mary and Maya, the Virgin and Shakti, once again run into one: and the Goddess is once more, as she ever was, the Creatress of the Universe, the self-revealing energy of the unknowable God.

So Mote it Be!

Application

When the Divine Feminine appears in your reading, it is most definitely a stark reminder that you, indeed, are, part of the distinguished line of Mothers/life givers/nurturers, right back to the very first Mother, that is in fact The Creatress of the Universe. When you realize you are not separate from, but ONE WITH the force that created our Universe, it truly puts you on notice that being a Woman is the greatest blessing of all blessings. That giving our power away is simply blasphemy.

This does not discount the male species, for being of both the fluids of a man and a woman, they too have a very strong feminine side. However...when one looks at the state of our world today, one has to wonder how this world would be shaped if Women were at the helm. Would there have been two world wars in our most recent history? As Marianne Williamson said in her address at the Washington Cathedral to an audience of Matriarchs, to the suggestion of War...."Not with our children you're not!"

We as Women must know our worth, our place and position in this world, our glory and our grace. If, every Woman on our planet agreed to not conceive another child until the male leaders of all those countries lay down their war toys and declare,

"Never again".......there would indeed be Peace on Earth.

From the North to the South,
From the West to the East,
Hear the prayers of the Mothers,
Bring them Peace, bring them Peace!

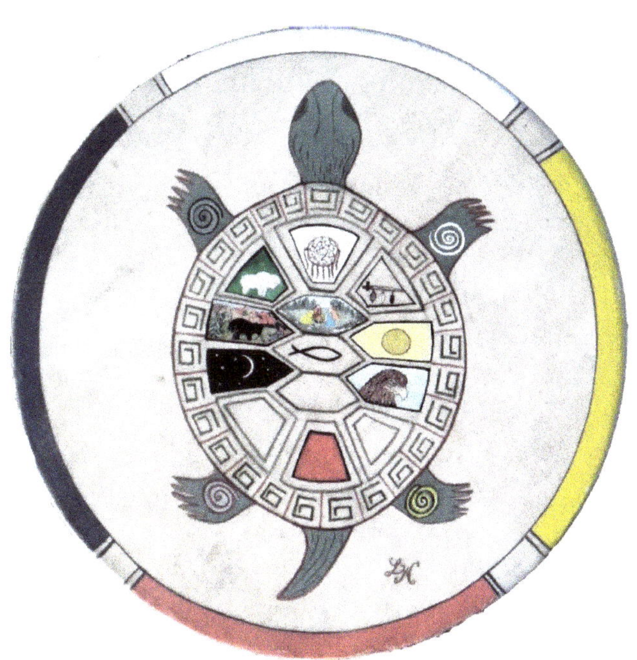

32. Crow

One of my own power animals is Crow. When I go on a Shamanic Journey Crow is always waiting for me at my starting place, often perched on my other power animal's antlers, Moose.

We have our own family of Crows at home here, and we feed them. We see them gathering sticks and grasses in the Spring, building their nests for their perspective fledglings. The prior family of fledglings, one year old's, generally stay close to help in the baby's raising, but at nightfall the yearlings head for the nearest town to places that are well lit, so that they can avoid the hunting owls through the night. In our nearby town there are so many crows gathering at night that you will see the trees covered in them, and on the roofs of buildings in the industrial park, and even on the ground....in great numbers. As the new fledglings grow, eventually the parents will bring them to our property, knowing that it is a good place to show them how to eat for themselves, and we always have morsels waiting for them. As a rule Crow is territorial and they keep it that way. Our family of Crows have been with us for thirty years.

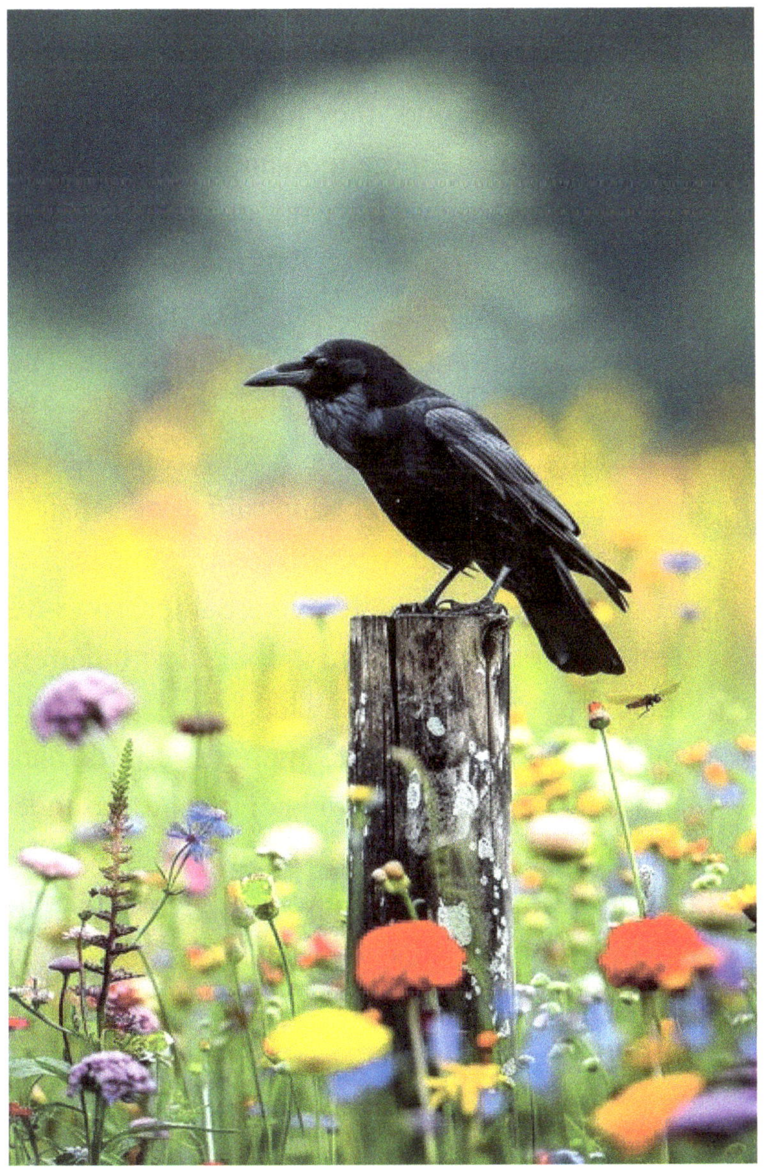

When we go for our walks in the woods, our Crows follow along, moving from tree top to tree top. They are very much aware of the places we stop at to share morsels of food for them.

Being rural Crows, they don't take chances and won't come down for the food until we start moving on, largely because we have our dogs with us. When we are in our house, and they arrive for their food, often they will make close swoops across our windows to remind us that it's time to eat! There was a time when my husband now, and I were best friends but not together yet as a couple, that he came to me in a dream one night and said to me, 'listen to Crows warnings and this will keep you safe.' The very next day while out in my yard, the Crows were literally screaming. I ran indoors...within a few minutes my 'x' drove by. This was a person that meant great harm to me, that the courts had a restraining order on. I heard later that he was indeed looking for an acquaintance out here that could loan him a gun! Fortunately that person did not give him one. That was close, too close! Thanks to Crow, and to me for listening, and to my best friend for warning me in that dream.

From the Native tradition, Crow is known as the shape shifter, the Shaman. Crow keeps one eye in ordinary reality and one eye in non ordinary reality at all times. According to John M. Marzluff and Tony Angell authors of 'In The Company of Crows and Ravens', Crows in any other area, wherever you are, will recognize you as people that feed Crows. Magical. Crow is one of the smartest birds in the world. Blessed Be.

Application

Choosing the Crow card in a Tarot reading is truly a gift to you. Crow indicates upcoming change or transformation, and beyond that, this refers more to a spiritual or emotional shift. These intelligent birds give us valuable insight into situations around us and help us adapt as necessary. You are being made aware, that listening to Crow is your greatest ally.

Finding a dead Crow generally indicates that the way you have been doing something, or your attitude or belief of something needs to die, for you to go on independently and at peace, otherwise, the affects of, for example, a recurring dream, will continue.

Crow has flown into your reading to comfort and sustain you. To help you see through any situation, clearly and meaningfully. Crow also offers to be with you in your awake time and in dream time.

We are a Circle, within a Circle,
With no beginning, and never ending.

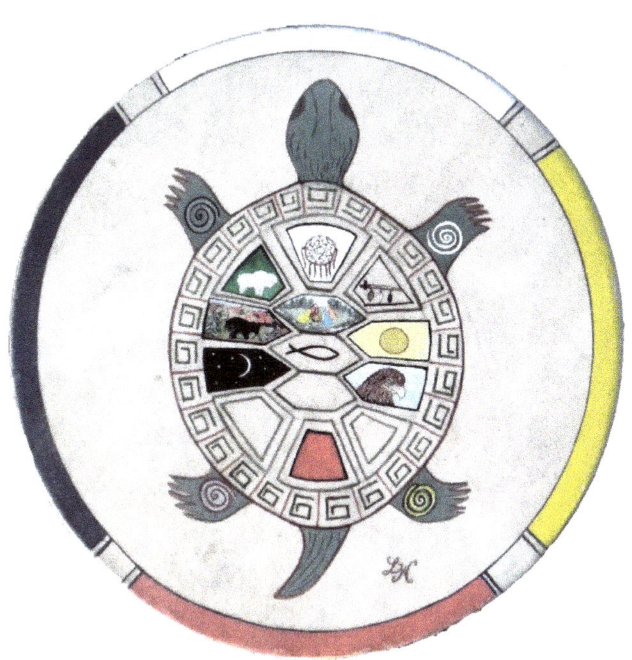

33. Smudging

In all our Women's Healing Circles, Drumming Circles and Workshops we begin with the sacred ceremony of Smudging. Cleansing our space and ourselves, using Sage, we remove any negative energy we may have gathered within our auras from negative people perhaps, or any negative places we may have unknowingly been in. We use dried Sage, known as a female herb, while Cedar is known as the male herb and Sweetgrass, known as the neutral herb.

In Mixed Healing Circles (men and women) generally I use Sage wrapped with Cedar. We light the Sage bundle and then blow out the flame, leaving the smoke flowing upward, bringing our intentions and our prayers up, to the Creator. We use an Abalone shell, being fireproof, to catch any embers. The shell brings in the element of 'Water', while the sage brings in the element of 'Earth', the flame brings in the element of 'Fire', and the smoke rising into the air, brings in the element of 'Air'. This is how we raise energy within our Circle.

Your Smudge can be offered to each of the four directions, then upward to Father Sky, and then downward to Mother Earth

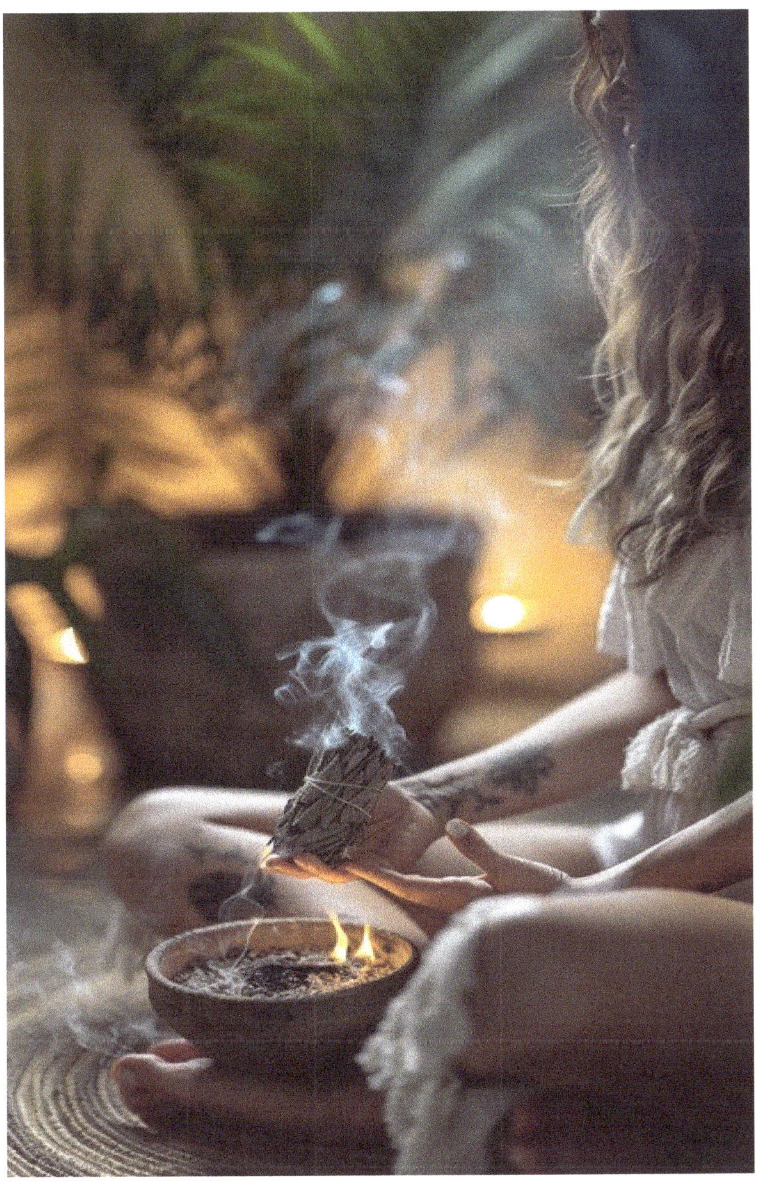

Passing the smoking sage bundle to my left, (the clockwise direction) I look into the eyes of the woman on my left and say, with great meaning, "I honor your journey, I honor your truth". This is repeated as the smudge is passed all the way around the Circle. If per chance I decide to smudge each woman myself, often I repeat the following:

You are a Being of Pure White Light,
You are a Being of Pure White Light,
Only Good can come to you,
Only Good can move through you,
Only Good can be here.

Blessed Be

Application

When the blessed card 'Smudging' has graced your reading, you are reminded to be mindful of the energies you pick up along your way, throughout your day, and bring into your home. Also, when you are using a space for your gatherings, you can smudge the space before anyone enters and/or smudge them when they enter, or let them smudge themselves....

The Sage bundle can be used in your Sweat Lodge before beginning....starting ceremony, with ceremony. If you are attending a Workshop weekend begin each segment of your weekend with Smudging. When doing so you may wish to bring the smoke, with your hands, up and over your head, or pass the vessel all around your body, back and front, fanning the smoke with a feather. Holding the vessel at your back will remove any anger you may hold.

To bring negative energy with you into your home presents unfinished business to your space, making you feel unsettled. Be gracious with yourself...taking time to cleanse, by Smudging to start and end every day. You will feel a change in your overall mood, your energy, and your attitude when approaching everyone you meet. In all cases, remember:

Not only are you the shadow that is dancing on the wall,
But you are the hand that makes the shadow,
And you are the Light.

May It Be So!

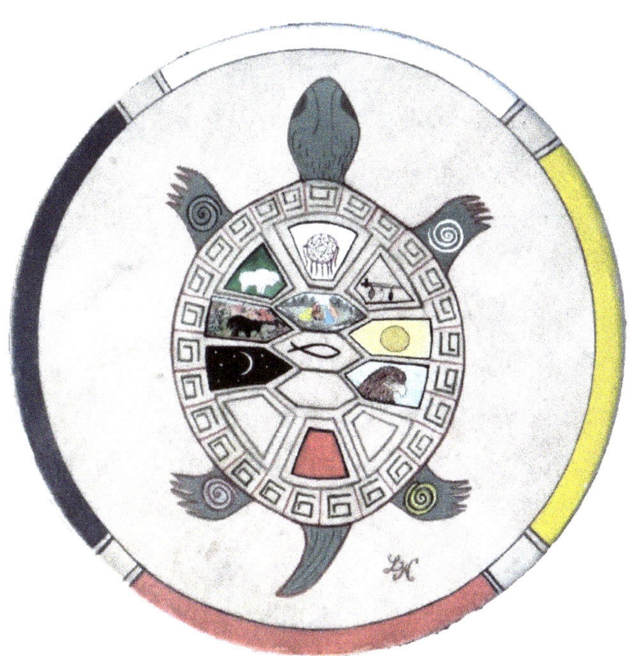

34. Addictions

My career included counselling at a Halfway House in Orillia Ontario for alcoholics coming off of skid row, and I had my own case load there. I also did the Group therapy program each day, and the AA meeting once a week. Following that I worked at the Addiction Research Foundation and started my own private practice as an Addictions Educational Consultant. Around that same time I was sexually assaulted by the son of a man I was with at the time. I went to counselling myself then, with Gloria Romanic M.A. and then joined her Woman's Healing Circle in Horseshoe Valley near Orillia, Ontario. Gloria's ideal was to see the women eventually branch out and start Women's Healing Circles in their own communities. It wasn't long before I started Healing Circles, after studying at Sir Sanford Fleming College, in Women's Studies, and eventually travelled to four other areas per week, to host these circles, which also included weekend workshops four times a year, on the Equinox's and Solstices.

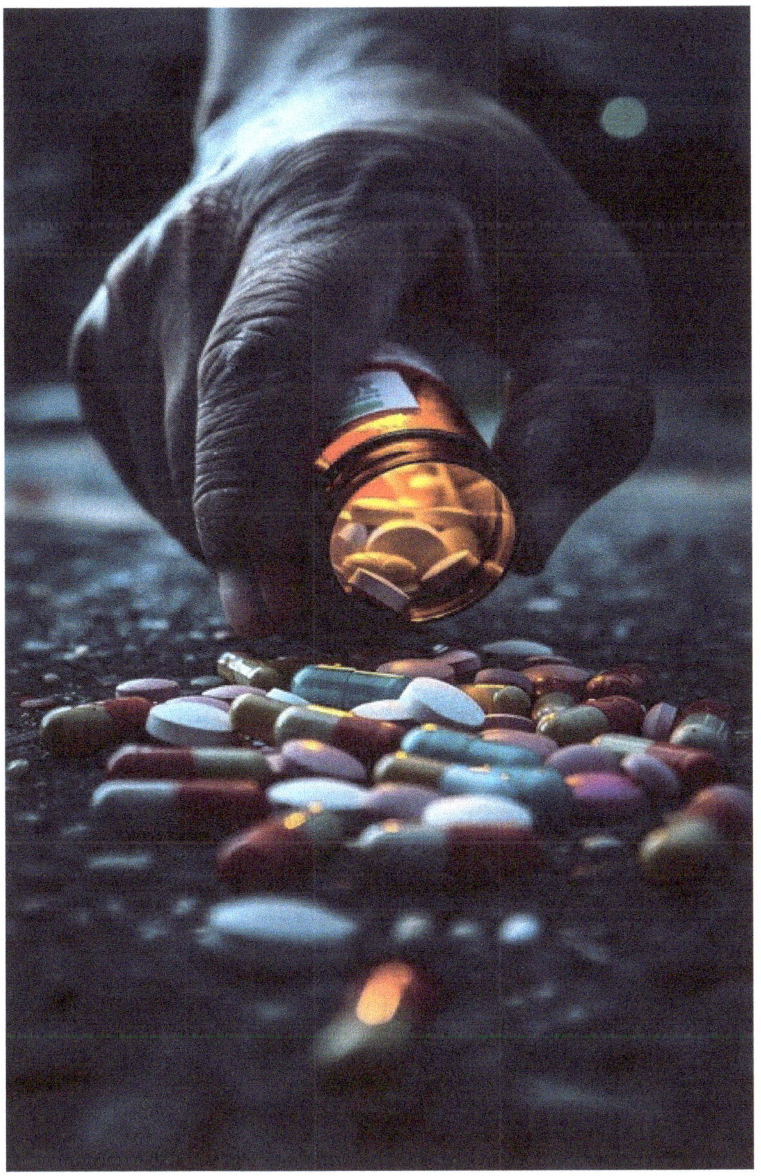

The Frederick House in Orilla, for youth also would call me to come in as a liaison to identify addictive substances some of the youths were using, and this was done after Frederick House's counselling staff had tried and failed to do so themselves. and this was done after Frederick House's counselling staff had tried and failed to do so themselves.

It isn't uncommon for an addict to shut down when speaking to a person that hadn't walked addiction themselves. Fortunately, this only took one appointment for me to identify the problem sources. I myself am a recovering alcoholic with fifty years sobriety. In my private practice, quite often a person would ask me at the beginning of their first appointment, how they would know, for sure, if they had a problem, or not. That was an easy question to answer. If, when they were under the influence of their choice of drug, did it ever cause even one problem? If the answer was yes, then we had a problem. Simple.

My Women's Healing Circles have continued here in Nova Scotia since I moved here in 1993. I also do Tarot Card readings by request. Not fortune telling,... but readings that speak to that which is going on in a person's life right now.

In my experience, in order for someone to change their life and completely sustain from their preferred substance, it boils down to being their choice. One either wants to be sober, identifying that they are powerless over the substance, or not. If a program is needed, then that's what they should do....by choice. As in all cases this decision, and sticking to it, is done, 'One Day at A Time'. Blessed Be.

Application

When the Addiction card appears in your reading, whether that be your own addiction or someone you know and love, the time is right to address it, now. Narcotics are especially difficult to break away from, but are doable with the right help. Nicotine has been said to be as hard to get away from as Opium, but again doable, yes, by choice. Alcohol too, affects not only the drinker but everyone and everything in their lives...and treatment is available.

The best way to stay sober from any substance is to replace it with a Spirituality that is one that speaks to you. One of your own, acquired by studying many, and coming home to make your own, whatever that is to you. The majority of cases I've worked with have proven to work best with a spirituality that is beyond Christianity. Not instead of, but as well as. A holistic model embraces mind, body and spirit...I encourage you to study any and ALL avenues of faith that speak to you.

Yoga and Meditation are also exceedingly helpful along with bringing in All That Is. You deserve to live in peace and in grace. If, like mine, your childhood was rough, fraught with an alcoholic parent or any other substance or even gambling, or sex addiction, this should be dealt with as well, in the same way as any other addiction is dealt with. Being whole is the goal, and choosing to be well is the way. Sobriety is admittedly a very selfish modality, but, sobriety MUST be number one, before anything, or anyone else, in your life. May It Be So.

Creator, Grant me the Serenity
To Accept the Things I cannot Change
The Courage to Change the things that I can
And the Wisdom, to know the Difference.

35. Vernal Equinox

The Vernal Equinox is a time when the daylight hours and night time hours are equal. Vernal means 'of the Spring' 'new' 'fresh' 'sap rising' 'Lady Earth Lives' and Equinox derived from the Latin aequus meaning equal and nox meaning night.

Spring! When all of the success achieved in last Autumn's harvest provides a road map to realize how and where we can benefit from the wisdom gained there, and what and when to plant in the Spring, bettering our outcome from last Spring's plantings. This is not only in terms of our gardens, but also in our every day lives. All these things pondered and planned all during the long Winter months.

Spring is a time of New Beginnings, of new life, of sprouting, of the return of the Light of the World, rebirth. The Vernal Equinox used to be known as the beginning of the New Year. Its moon bound celebration Easter was named originally for the Saxon Goddess Eostre who gave her name to Easter.

This Sabbat celebrates the return of Persephone from the underground, to her Mother Demeter who once again awakens all sleeping seeds.

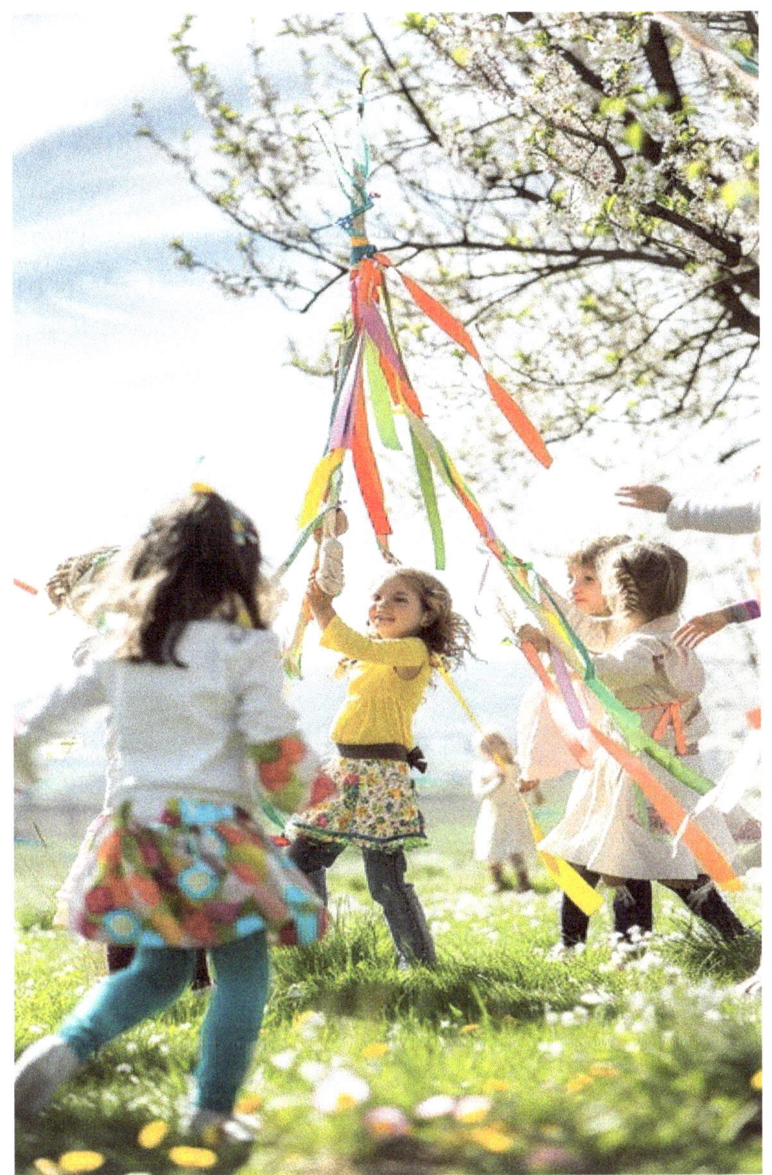

Vernal Equinox decorations center around the warming of the Earth, and the renewal of her fertility; seeds sprouting in the darkness, after a winter of dormancy; and the rising of the Spring constellations in the night sky. Appropriate decorations are budding twigs, crocuses, willow catkins, the first shoots of grasses, or wheat sprouts in an earthenware pot, like the famous "Gardens of Adonis" that women planted each year for the resurrection of Eostre's vegetation god.

We all come from the Goddess
And to her we shall return
Like a drop of water
Flowing to the Ocean

Application

This Tarot card has great meaning for you right now. A time of New Beginnings...great changes in your life. Whether this be about relationships or career changes, or planning for a child in your life, etc. This is the time to plant your dreams and desires to manifest into being. Last year's harvest has shown you where you can better your world, in all ways.

Decorate your home with reminders of this time of rebirth, journal your thoughts and feelings daily, take a class, join a Women's Healing Circle, bask in the hopes and dreams you've brought to your world thus far, and keep moving forward.

Look for the signs in the wild to guide you to become all you were created to be. Soaring eagles, fluttering butterflies, nesting birds, awakening hibernators, the return of migrating birds, budding sprouts, sap flowing. Above all else be gentle with your dear self. May It Be So!

36. Summer Solstice – National Indigenous Peoples Day

In the South position on the Medicine Wheel, the season is Summer representing rapid growth. The Sun has reached its most Northernly position. National Indigenous Peoples Day is celebrated on the Summer Solstice. As the longest day of the year, and the shortest night, the Summer Solstice holds deep cultural and spiritual significance for most Indigenous peoples. It symbolizes a new season of life, a chance to start fresh and leave past burdens behind.

In Pagan communities 'one' of the rituals held is to jump over campfires as high as they can jump to symbolize the height of the crops for the year. The Native Sun Symbol represents life-giving abundance with its warmth radiating healing and peace. The sun was freed and given back to the earth by the Raven, who released it out of its confining box. Since then it has given all humankind warmth, light, and life.

The Summer Solstice marks the onset of summer, and it's a cause for celebration. Each solstice thousands of people head to Stonehenge, which is famous for its alignment on sunrise on the special day.

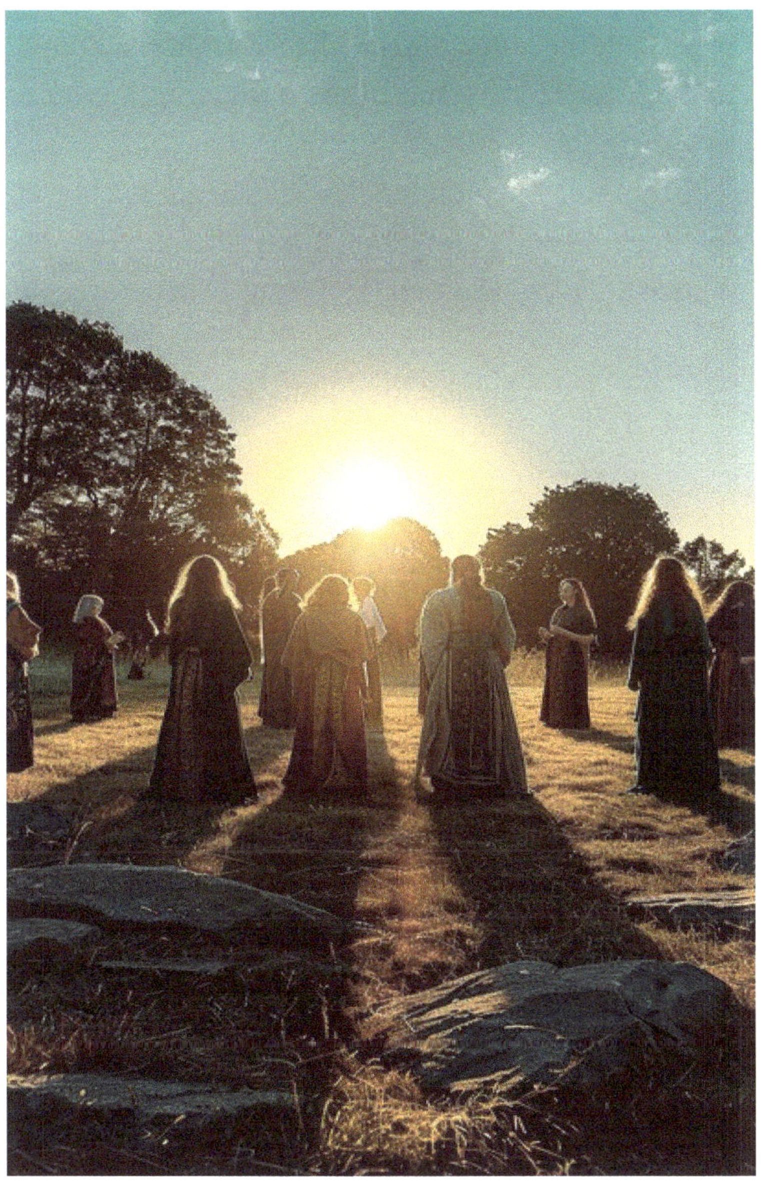

Standing in the centre of the monument at Summer Solstice, the sun rises just to the left of a large standing stone outside the stone circle, known as the Heel Stone, seen through a gap in the outer sarsen circle.

From this day onward the days begin to shorten once again, until the shortest day of the year, the Winter Solstice. Blessed Be!

May the long time Sun
Shine upon you
All love surround you
And the pure light, within you
Guide your way on
Guide your way on.

Snatam Kaur

Application

The Summer Solstice card has fallen into your hands this day as a true blessing. Get up out of bed and stretch and greet the sun, every day, all year long and if the sun isn't shining for you, greet the daylight. Enjoy nature's bounty always. Bring life to something. Light a fire, and if that isn't doable, light a candle. Immerse yourself in water. Celebrate your life every day. Repeat three things you are grateful for, every morning. Send Love and Light to everyone you know and love.

Refresh and nourish your body...your temple. The Summer Solstice is a time of diminishing light every day until the Winter Solstice...celebrate!

Traditionally the Summer Solstice is a time for celebrating. It's the lightest 'yang' time of the year and a time to celebrate the light, life, and ourselves. This is a very potent time for birthing new energy, new beginnings, manifesting, and welcoming in abundance too. Simply go outside and extend your arms out, and upward receiving abundance.

Smudge yourself saying:

You are a being of Pure White Light,
You are a being of Pure White Light,
Only Good can come to you,
Only Good can move through you,
Only Good can be here.

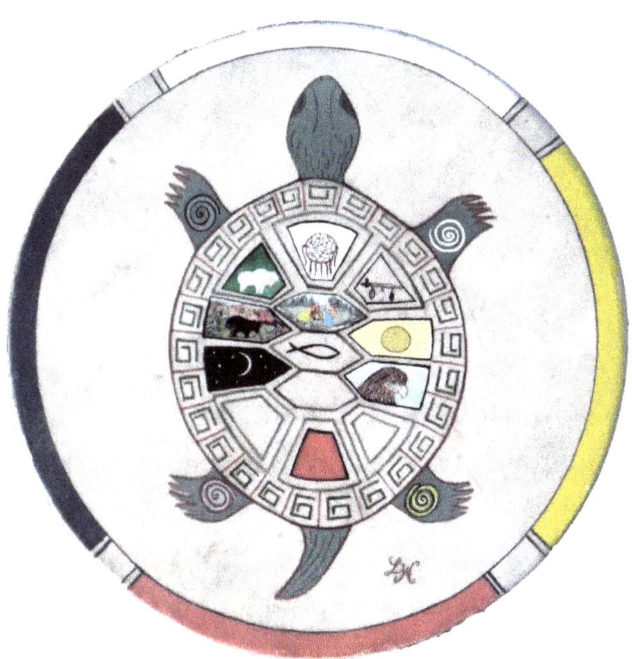

37. Autumn Equinox

I'm not sure that there is a prettier time of year than Autumn and I am blessed to be living in a place that gives me four seasons each year. The glorious colours, not only in our leaves but also in the sky's golden glow. Autumn is the time of the Harvest. All our plannings and plantings in the Spring lay before us in all its glory. The New Beginnings that we put in motion in Spring are here for us in this glorious season of Autumn. A time to go within, like bear retreating to its den for its long winter's sleep. The first day of Autumn brings peace and wisdom.

During the autumnal equinox, the sun shines directly on the equator, while the northern and southern hemispheres get the same amount of rays. Spiritually, this seasonal change is related to growth and expansion. Gratitude, prosperity and cleansing are the main drivers for small rituals or ceremonies to fill and prepare your mind for good energies. Cleansing our minds, homes and bodies.

It indicates a moment of stillness before the Earth shifts directions. The fall equinox is a sacred day of equal parts of light and dark, facing outward as well as turning inward, and allowing our past and future to merge in the present.

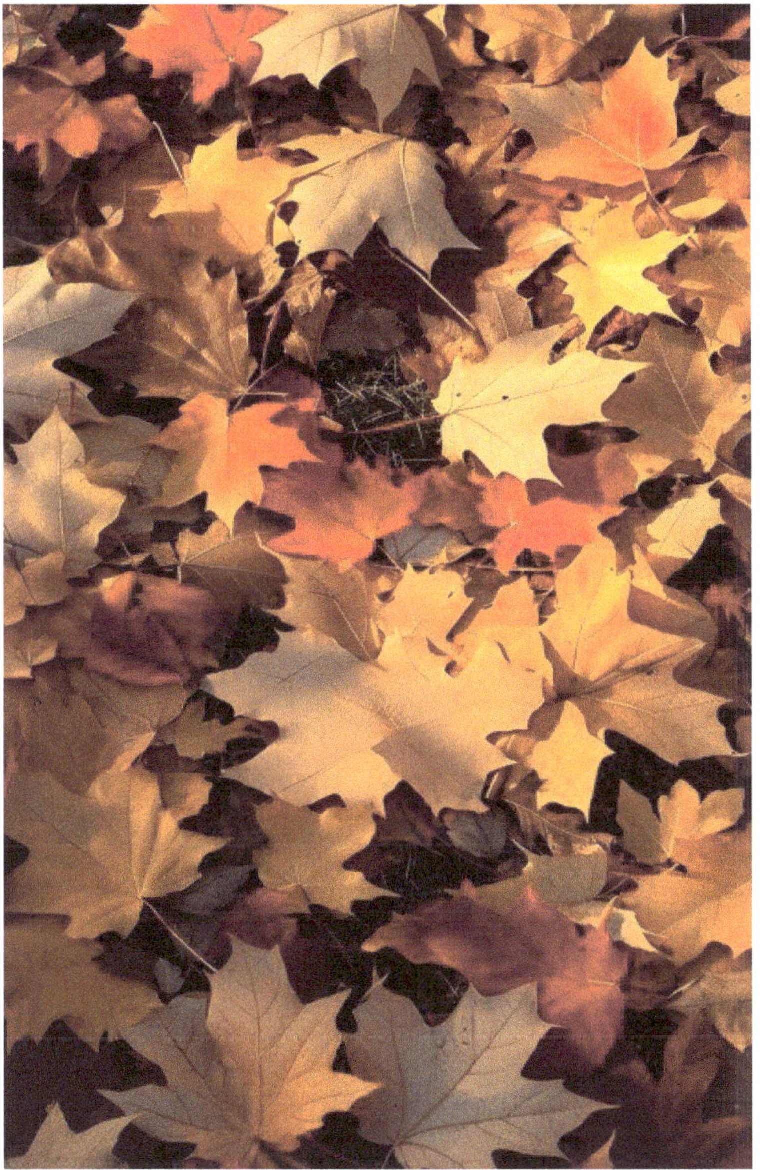

I remember vividly, a time when my own Daughter moved from the province we raised her in, to another province many miles away. I was devastated and wondered how I would go on without her and her son, my first grandson, near to me. After speaking to a colleague about how I was (not) dealing with this change, she reminded me that this too was the time of the year, the Autumn Equinox, when Demeter, the Mother Goddess, had to face the absence of her Daughter Persephone when the God of the Underground, Hades, took her away, stating that Persephone would have to stay with him. Demeter grieved mercifully, and froze the Earth hard, killing all vegetation, proclaiming that nothing would grow again, until her Daughter was returned to her. Hades told Persephone that he would bring her back to Demeter in the Spring, but if Demeter greeted her Daughter by asking her if she was hungry, she would have to go back with him in the Autumn once again until the next Spring. Indeed when Hades brought Persephone back in the Spring, the nurturing mother Demeter, ran to her, holding out her arm with a pomegranate in her hand saying, 'oh my dear Daughter...I'm so happy to see you...are you hungry?' The land again turned green and the sap ran once more, and the flowers bloomed, and the birds sang. But....this meant that the God of the Underground came back every Autumn to get Persephone again, promising he would return her in the Spring, forever more.

My Daughter did in fact return to me once again, but only for a short while, and she returned to the province she moved to before.....and I followed.

Application

When the Autumn Equinox card dances into your reading you are reminded to:

Clear Up Space: It is the time to clean your home, throw or give away unwanted things or emotional associations that hold you back. Burn sage to clear your space, wash your crystals and let them charge under the harvest full moon, ring some bells to clear out the psychic dust.

When you learn to explore deeply, you uncover your true power & gifts and are able to find meaning in your past failures. This is when you begin to believe in yourself again, and that is when you become powerful beyond belief.

As we consciously link our awareness to the cycles of nature, our understanding of our own cycles begins to deepen.

You may want to honor all that you have in your life and shift your consciousness from one of lack to one of prosperity and gratitude in some way through a small ritual or ceremony. Such as lighting a candle, giving thanks, and speaking your gratitude for all that you have, all that you are, and all you are created to be. May It Be So.

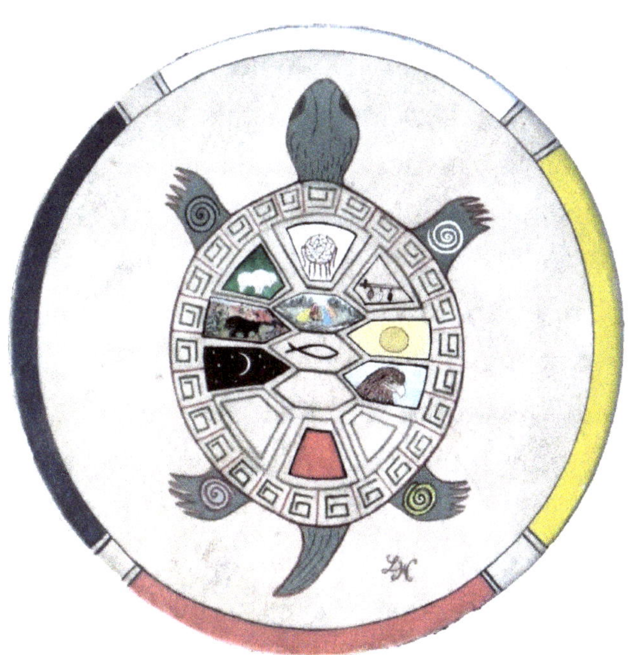

38. Midwinter Solstice

On this day, the sun is at its lowest point in the sky, travelling across the sky world above us in a short stride, resulting in the shortest day and the longest night of the year in the Northern Hemisphere. From this day forward the days lengthen, and for this we are exceedingly happy. In ancient times people would wonder if the days would ever get longer again, and this caused considerable anxiety, and they prayed to their Gods that the days would begin to lengthen, because then they could plan their plantings and restore their food reserves, for certain. (In Northern countries the onset of doomsday was believed to be marked by continuous winter for three full years.)

During the darkest months of the year, it was said that this was a time that tribal Elders weren't busy, either planting, or harvesting and had time to counsel those that came to them to gain their wisdom. When you went to and Elder for advice it was advisable to follow it, and not to ignore or squander their wisdom. Otherwise you may not be offered that chance again.

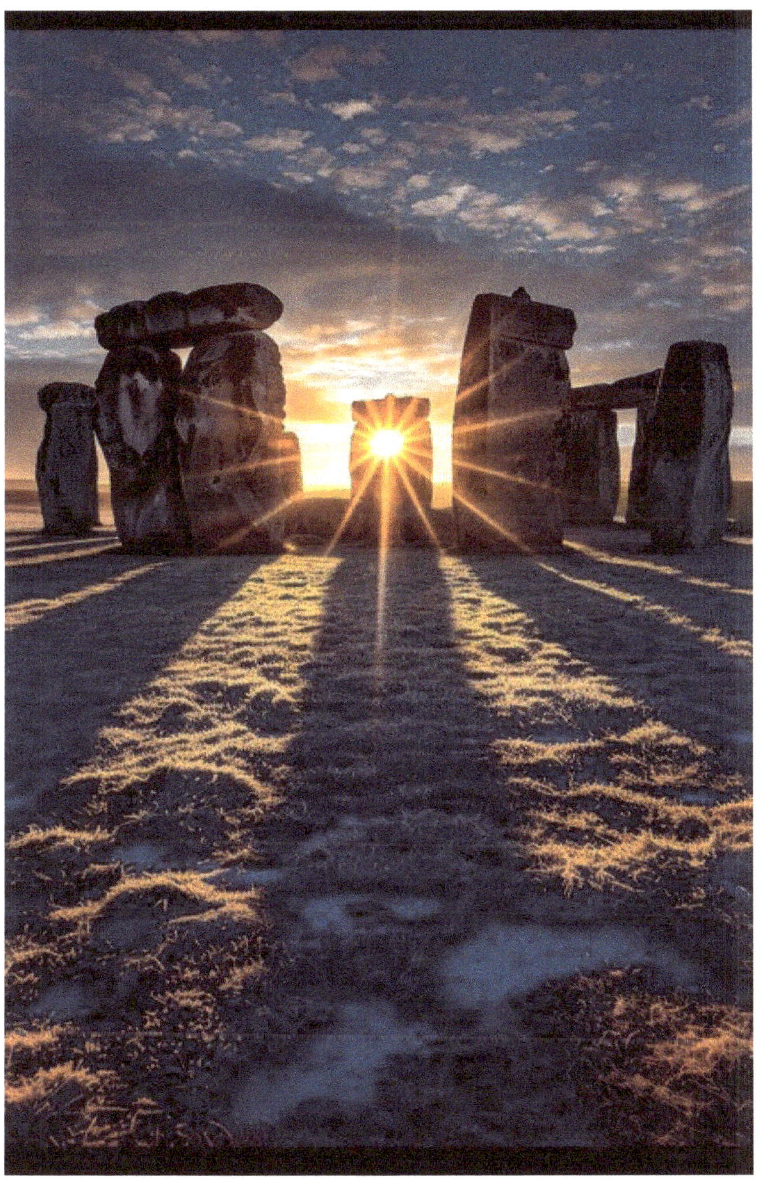

Indigenous peoples everywhere observe the Winter Solstice. It is the day that the sun is the furthest from the equator. Their spiritual foundation lies in the natural world of connection and Solstice is a time to honour and acknowledge the natural patterns of our Universe and existence.

Holly is a highly appropriate decoration for this festival because it was adopted from the Pagan Yule and was originally named for the dark underground Crone-Goddess Holle, or Hel, from whose womb the sun arose. The red berries of the holly symbolized the Goddess's holy blood, shaper of all life, according to the oldest beliefs. England still has many "Hollywells" or "Holywells" once considered yonic shrines of this Goddess. The evergreen leaves of the holly represented ongoing life, retaining vitality through the Winter, with an implied promise of immortality.

Our Circles today gather for celebrations on the night of the Winter Solstice, and one way was by lighting up a tree outdoors together, each with their own (supplied) light bulb to do so.

Who are the Witches
Where do they come from?
Maybe your Great Great Grandmother was one.
Witches are wise wise Women they say,
And there's a little Witch in every Woman today!

Application

The Midwinter Solstice card is a reminder to us to celebrate the ongoing blessings of our Universe's celestial events and their meanings in our lives. Not just on the days of the Solstices and Equinox's but always. Be generous with your celebrations and gift yourself with giving praise and thanks for these teachings. Create your altars in such a way that they can be filled with replicas of ancient ways, and also of current traditions. Altars are sacred and speak of your trust in all ways of the Earth and her company that dances with her in the cosmos. You will then be in harmony with our Moon's cycles, the Sun, the Stars and our beautiful home, Mother Earth.

It's not possible for our human brains to conceive the vastness of the Universe that has created, and continues to create. But our place within the Milky Way and our own galaxy is something you can relate to.

On the Solstices and Equinox's dress in your favourite regalia, or in nothing at all, and dance in the Full Moon light. Celebrate that we are all capable of finding the North Star and then standing or dancing in the center of the Universe. These are the ways to bring peace and happiness to your heart, always, and to live as we are meant to live, in Love and Respect for all. May It Be So!

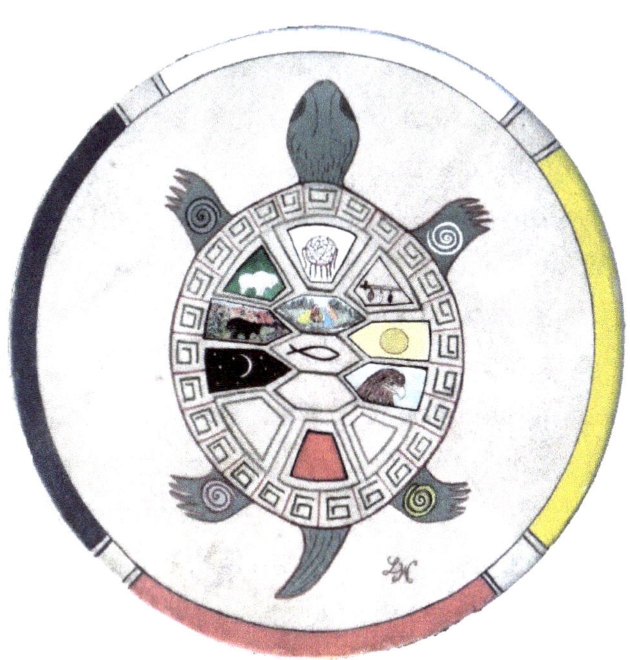

39. Crystals

Shamans usually choose a clear Crystal to carry on their person. This in no way is saying that a quartz crystal with fractures in it is any less powerful. Quartz Crystals store energy, your energy. They can be recharged by setting them outside on the Full Moon, or running clear spring water over them, or burying them in a container of sand.

Crystals are also used in home cleansing prior to moving in, and for protection. In a home cleansing you would use a sage bundle and when you have it smoking nicely, enter each room moving from corner to corner, and even in the closets. When the entire home is smudged you would use a broom to sweep out any negative energy that was in the home before you moved in. Four Crystals can then be placed in the ground at the four directions, with the pointed end facing in toward the home. This method not only cleanses the home but protects it also.

Crystals can also be used by programming them, carrying one on your person with yours, or the needs of someone else's intention within it. You would meditate over the crystal, informing it of the matter at hand and carry it with you for as long as the intention takes to manifest.

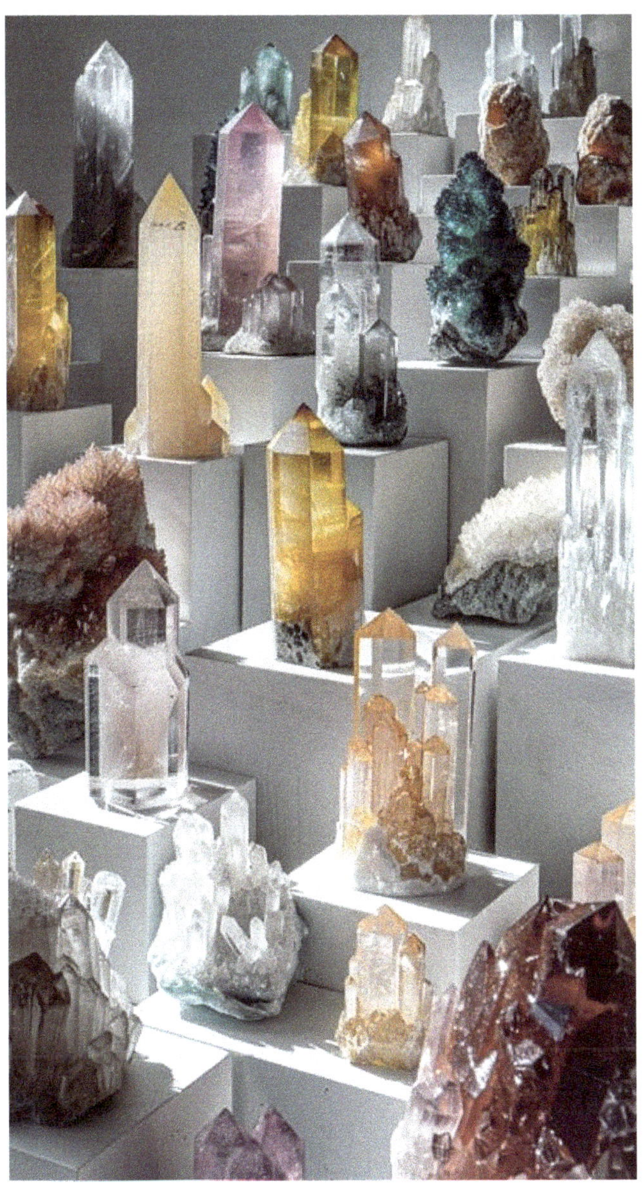

Always cleanse the Crystal once the work is completed. Only good will be answered by the Crystal...never ill intent.

Crystals are most likely the most popular trends used in alternative medicine, having the power to heal physical ailments and illnesses. They have been used in the UK for protection and well being as far back as 10,000 years ago. Apparently Leonardo da Vinci reportedly kept a gemstone on his desk, claiming, an Amethyst Crystal dispels evil thoughts and speeds up thinking. So Mote It Be.

When we are gone,
They will remain,
Wind and rock,
Fire and Rain,

They will remain
When we return
The winds will blow
And the fires will burn.

Application

The rock and mineral kingdom are not unlike herbal remedies, or any other healing practices here on our planet.

The tools for healing, including herbs, are many, that have been graciously given to us by our Mother the Earth, and of course the Creator of all things in our Universe that has created, and continues to create. Don't be shy about adding these tools to your healing journey....not excluding Western Medicines.

Should your focus while coming to your Tarot deck today be your own healing or the healing of someone you love, know that you enhance that healing using alternative means, that have been used for millennia.

Offer every chance you can to yourself and others, that have been used scientifically, for thousands of years, because you deserve everything that is available to you. Gratitude and prayer, supported by the tools of well being on Earth only enhance your intentions. May It Be So.

40. Death

There are a multitude of reasons why some people refuse to go to Fortune Tellers or Psychics but the foremost reason in my experience is fear. The fear of hearing something bad, either about themselves or someone they care for. This is understandable because there are people that practice Fortune Telling that do indeed deliver such news to those they read for. I wanted to have the opportunity to speak to this subject from my own perspective.

I believe that anyone that would instill fear by giving such a reading to anyone should brace themselves. Giving such a reading to anyone only brings bad luck to the reader. In fact, in my work I make it a practice to reassure people that I have been doing readings for decades, and have never nor will I ever do such a thing. I believe that when you are working in the light you don't even see such things. I also reassure people that I am NOT a Fortune Teller.

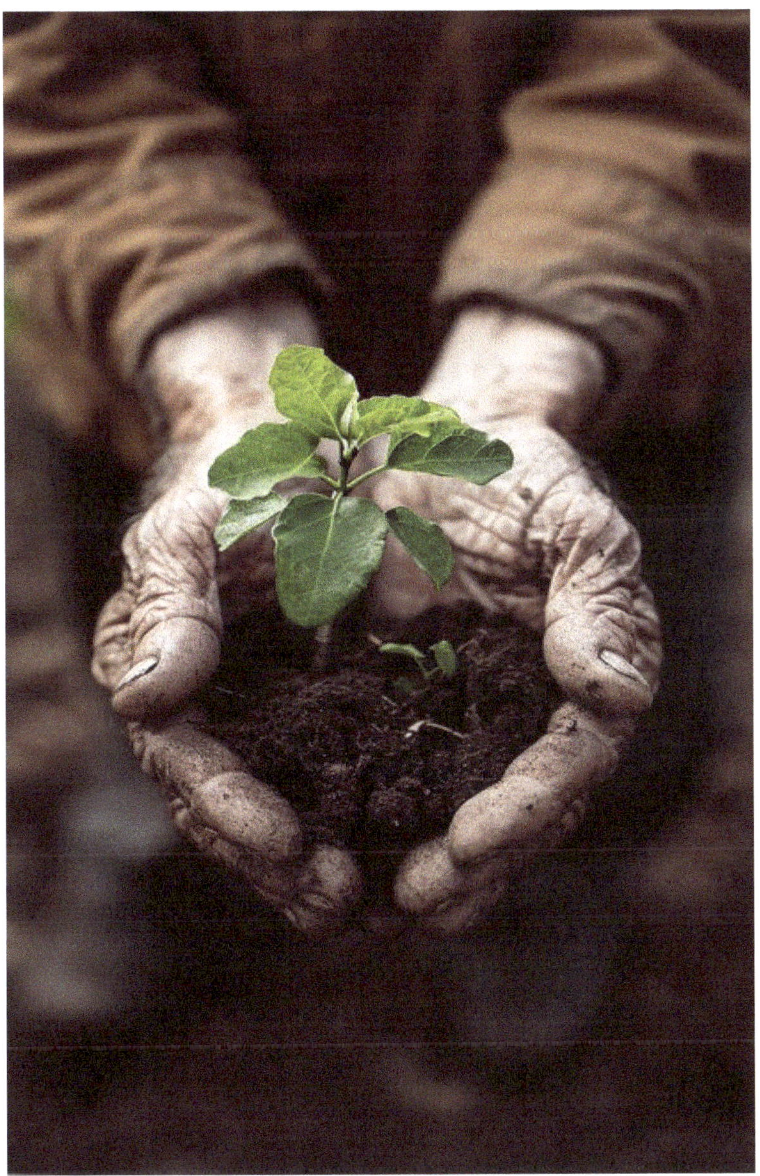

The readings I do speak to what is going on in a persons life right now, in the present moment, giving insight and guidance and making sure those that I read for understand that it is not I that has any sort of power....that it is they that have that blessing. If when going into a reading you can clear the clutter along the pathway from your heart, and the heart of the force that created you, clutter being, for example: where you are going after your reading, or, your shopping list, or any such mundane clutter...If when going into a reading you can clear the clutter along the pathway from your heart, and the heart of the force that created you, clutter being, for example: where you are going after your reading, or, your shopping list, or any such mundane clutter...the clearer your reading will be. That if you go into your reading with 'focus' on the matter that will address what is going on for you right now 'only,' your reading will be bang on. I simply provide the tools and the guidance in terms of interpreting the reading.

The old Rider-Waite Tarot would be an example, in my opinion, of a Tarot I wouldn't touch and is on the same level as the Ouija Board for me. I wouldn't have such a thing in my possession. That said, my interpretation of the Death card is as follows:

When the Death card is chosen in a reading it means that some aspect of you, or an aspect of your life is about to end, to die, to change...making room for a new way of seeing things, replacing the way you once saw or did things...That will improve your life, and the lives of everyone and everything you have always known to be true, and that once served you well. And now, this new path, be it an alternative way of knowing and believing, will serve you much better. This is the truth. My truth. May It Be So!

Application

When you draw the Death card from this Tarot Deck, completely written in the light, you are being put on notice that things are about to change in a big way in your world, and in the world around you. This positive reading brings you great news, great relief, great change. You can say goodbye to outdated conditioning, for this farewell will provide you with positive insight. You have hit the jackpot!

It is not uncommon to lapse back into old ways of knowing, because of its familiarity, albeit somewhat destructive. But you will now identify the darkness this old conditioning brings, by how it feels within you, and you will immediately choose a new positive light, in every and all cases.

You will show this enlightenment not only on your face, but in your stride, and you will draw goodness to you, in all ways. This change will present not unlike a shield that is ever and always worn like a Spiritual Warrior. Congratulations, and may Blessings abound.

So Mote It Be!

May the Circle be Open, yet Unbroken
May the Love of the Goddess be ever in our Hearts
Merry Meet and Merry Part
And Merry Meet Again!
Blessed Be

www.ingramcontent.com/pod-product-compliance
Ingram Content Group UK Ltd.
Pitfield, Milton Keynes, MK11 3LW, UK
UKHW021831270726
14058UKWH00001B/83